BROUGHT

By

Andrew Cook

"I remember saying.... I'd expose the devil to as many as would listen before I went"

'Four Funerals and a Revelation' © Cook, AW 2006

Prologue.

> "There are two equal and opposite errors into which our race can fall about the devils.'One is to disbelieve in their existence. The other is to believe, and to feel an excessive and unhealthy interest in them. They themselves are equally pleased by both errors and hail a materialist or a magician with the same delight"
> – C.S. Lewis, The Screw tape Letters

I thought it was important to mention the fall of Satan at the beginning of this book, to show where the notion of Absinthe derives from. It's quite easy for me to imagine peace, love, joy and harmony in heaven, disrupted by one presumptuous angel who gets too big for his boots and starts to desire all the praise and glory for himself. This pride gets him ostracised and the angels have free will to choose sides and stay or go, a third of them went. It seemed fitting as well that Acqua should change his name to Absinthe just as Lucifer's name was changed to Satan.

As a counsellor working with the psychological, talk of demons would generally be frowned upon. As a Christian though I cannot and will not interpret the word of God as an analogy or fairy story. Satan does exist, if you believe the word and consequently, so do the demons. Who talks about Satan nowadays? Not many people. When we do it's usually in a joking way. Satan was originally known as Lucifer. Lucifer was the anointed Cherub, set apart for God's divine purpose. Just imagine being God's "top dog". Lucifer was God's top dog but pride got the better of him and he sinned. Consequently Lucifer got booted out of Heaven for his pride and for trying to be better than God.

"12 How you have fallen from heaven, morning star, son of the dawn! You have been cast down to the earth, you who once laid low the nations! 13 You said in your heart I will ascend to the heavens; I will raise my throne above the stars of God; I will sit enthroned on the mount of assembly, on the utmost heights of Mount Zaphon 14 I will ascend above the tops of the clouds; I will make myself like the Most High."

Isaiah 12-15

He wasn't prepared to go quietly or alone so war broke out in Heaven and Lucifer took his angels with him,

"Then war broke out in heaven and his angels fought against the dragon and the dragon and his angels fought back. 8 But he was not strong enough and they lost their place in heaven. 9 The great dragon was hurled down-that ancient serpent called the devil, or Satan, who leads the whole world astray. He was hurled to the earth, and his angels with him."

Revelations 12:7-9

Lucifer became Satan and his angels now became known as demons. Satan must have landed on earth after God created Adam and Eve on day six of creation because up until then god's creation was "good", God obviously found out what had been going on and Adam and Eve where faced now with serious consequences. Kicked out of Eden to faced a life of separation from God, hard graft painful child birth and of course - death (Genesis 3:16-19. Satan was forewarned it's: not over yet he will crush your head and you will strike his heel" Genesis 3-15. As I mentioned early, here God is hinting at the Messiah who will come to save us from our sin and destroy Satan's power over those who believe. Life was no walk in the park from then on for Adam and Eve. Their first traumatic experience, after their eviction was losing their son Abel who was murdered by his own brother Cain.

Cain was then cursed by God to live a life of misery. His crops were to bare him no fruit and nobody was to kill him.

Time went by and Satan continued his exploits, enticing men into all sorts of sins. Eventually God got sick of it and decided to have a fresh start and get rid of the human race, however, God still saw favour in one man - Noah. God spared Noah and his family and the human race and effectively started again from Noah as the rest of man was wiped from the face of the earth.

Moses wrote the Torah Law for the people of Israel at the time of the Exodus from Egypt and when the Israelites got to Mount Sinai God laid the law down to them in black and white in a very public way by appearing on the mountain. From then on the law was clear cut. The Law would help people to understand the depth of their sinfulness (in that they were incapable of keeping the Law) so that they might more readily accept the cure for that sin through the coming messiah Jesus. They were incapable of keeping the law because Satan, from the time of Adam and Eve's disobedience to some unknown time in the future is "god of this age".

"The god of this age has blinded the minds of unbelievers, so that they cannot see the light of the gospel that displays the glory of Christ, who is the image of God. " 2 Corinthians 4:4

God saw our inability to adhere to his law and in his mercy sent us a savior and a King. God in His mercy saw what we are up against "the god of this world" and knows Satan and what he is capable of.

So our Savior was born with a humble beginning.

7 "and she gave birth to her first born, a son. She wrapped him in cloths and placed him in a manger, because there was no guest room available for them". Luke 2:7

Satan did his best to try and get Jesus to bow down to him but Jesus was having none of it. Satan new his days were numbered.

Though Satan remains "god of this age" for the time being, the death and resurrection of Jesus has rendered him powerless in the lives of believers.

"He will crush your head, and you will strike his heel"
Genesis 3-15

So now we jump forward to the 20th Century. Satan defeated by the cross, knows his days are numbered. So what better way to make the most of a bad situation than to convince the world that you don't exist and that is exactly what happened in the 20th Century thanks to theologians such as Rudolf Bultmann and the Theory of Demythologization? A seed was planted that today in 2012 renders talk about such things as Satan and demons as foolish and comical.

In modern times Satan continues his war against God. Anton Szandor founded the church of Satan in San Francisco in 1966. From 1960 to 1966 he developed his satanic philosophy. He viewed the devil as a dark force hidden in nature, ruling earthly affairs. Man's true nature he claimed, is one of lust pride, hedonism and wilfulness, attributes that he claimed enable the advancement of civilisation. He claimed that flesh should not be denied but celebrated. Individuals who stand in the way of achieving what one wants should be cursed, according to La Vey.

Chapter 1

Before the beginning.

Lucifer is an archangel in God's kingdom, not only that he is God's chief body guard. He enjoys a very high position in the spiritual realms and God holds him in very high esteem. He is greatly loved. His friends in heaven include Gaudium (Latin name for Happiness,) Animus (Latin name for courage), Insontis (Latin name for Innocence), Acqua, Sanctimonia (Latin name for Purity) and Vita (Latin name for Life).

These angels enjoy a privileged position in God's kingdom. They devote their lives to serving and praising the Lord. Every day the hosts of angels can be heard singing beautiful songs and creating beautiful music that is pleasing to the Lord's ear.

Lucifer and his friends have no limits on where they can go. They travel through the whole of god's creation and marvel at its beauty and glory. Everything is wonderful and pure and just how it should be.

Over time Lucifer develops quite a following amongst his friends. He is always applauded and praised when the angels gather to worship the Lord.

God was creating a new planet that would be very special to him, very special. On day one he separated the darkness from the light on earth. Lucifer assisted by helping to move the sun into position. He was very pleased with himself that he had done such a good job at helping.

On day two Lucifer assisted in creating the sky and in separating morning from evening. The angels started to look in awe at how wonderful Lucifer was and he revelled in the attention that he was getting. God saw this and he was concerned but said nothing at that time.

On day three God put trees plants and vegetation on the earth. Lucifer again helped out and relished the praise he got for his hard work and strength. He started to see himself as better than all the other angels. God was not happy about this but said nothing.

On the fourth day God made the sun, moon and stars. He did not ask Lucifer to help him on the fourth day; instead he put one of the lesser angels in charge. Lucifer got wind of this and was jealous and hurt that he had not been asked. He got angry with God.

On the fifth day God created the living creatures, the sea creatures and the birds. Lucifer was not asked again, but now he was busy plotting to set himself up as better than God, telling all the angels to praise him and not God. God knew but kept quiet.

On the sixth day God created man from the dust of the earth. He created man in his own image and gave him permission to rule over the fish in the sea and the birds in the sky and over every living creature. God said that it was good.

Satan was furious that God had created them in his own image and was jealous. He defiantly lifted himself up above the stars and called on the multitude of angels to worship him instead of God. The angels quickly segregated into two groups - the faithful two thirds that were reviled by Lucifer's nerve to even think that he could be better than God and the third that fatally chose to follow him.

A disagreement started to emerge in the heavens as the faithful angels beckoned the others to see reason and return before God came back from Earth and it was too late.

On the seventh day God rested on earth. He just chilled out, paddled in the sea, chatted to Adam and Eve, told them which tree not to eat from and had a thoroughly enjoyable day after the six days of hard work. He enjoyed chatting with Adam and Eve about what they could call all the animals.

On the eighth day god woke up early with a serious look on his face. He knew exactly what was going on back in heaven and after saying goodbye to Adam and Eve went back to his heavenly throne. God saw what was going on.

"Lucifer get down from there, what are you playing at?"

"I'm better than you now God, look, look how many of your angels have chosen to worship me now!"

"Get out now! And take your followers with you then!" God

throws Lucifer and his followers (totalling a third of the angels) out of heaven and they fall down and land on the earth.

Once they have recovered from the fall they start to get their bearings.

In heaven God decrees that from now on the fallen angels will be known as demons. Lucifer will be called Satan, Gaudium will be called Desparus

Animus will be called Metus, Insontis will be called Culpus, Acqua will be called Absinthe, Sanctimonia will be called Lustus and Vita will be called Suicidus.

They started to explore the earth and see how beautiful it was. Many of the demons would have been happy for things to remain as they were, after all it was peaceful and quiet, but Satan had other ideas. He now had a score to settle with God and wanted revenge. As they travelled around the earth one of the demons discovered the Garden of Eden and informed Satan that he had found these "human things". Satan came to see for himself.

"Well, well, look at that! He made them in His image did he!" said Satan.

"Desparus, I bet he told them not to eat the fruit from that tree. Look! See how they won't go near it. She's dying to try it, look at her! Hey why don't you go and persuade her to eat it!"

"Mmmh, I might just do that!"

And so begins the story of the fall of man. As you may already know Adam and eve did eat the fruit from that tree and Satan perverted the beautiful thing God had created that he once called "good".

God forewarned Satan in the Garden of Eden,

> "He will crush your head,
>
> and you will strike his heel."
>
> Genesis 3:15

that a saviour would come, God's son, to save those who accept him as Lord and Saviour and indeed he did come and Satan was defeated at Calvary but remained prince of this world until -

Chapter 2

The Return of Jesus

Earth, 2048 - in the months after the return of Jesus. The final years before his return were the worst the world has ever seen with devastation, starvation, ugly wars, oppression and one world leader who had the nerve to call himself God. The world was a black, nasty place to be. When the asteroid hit in 2012 it wiped out a third of the world's water supply and millions of people died of poisoning from drinking it.

As promised, Jesus came years later though when everyone least expected it. His followers had already been taken away by then. They just disappeared, as though they had just been lifted into the clouds.

When he came back he wasn't the same meek and gentle Jesus that left the earth two thousand or so years previously. People were first alerted by a trumpet call and shout which rang through the ears of every remaining person on the earth. There was no donkey; he entered through the cloud on a white stallion. Its mane was long and silver. He was carrying a sword and accompanied by a multitude of angels and when I say a multitude I mean millions of them, all in ranks. They lit up the sky silver and gold as they descended to earth. Their first destination was Jerusalem, which was under attack from armies from all four corners of the world, at the time.

The angels wiped out the armies attacking Jerusalem in a short but gruesome battle. As the world armies neared defeat a demon appeared from nowhere - Satan. He faced up to Jesus head on; he was no ordinary angel though. He was seething angry but scared at the same time. It took out a whole platoon of Jesus' angels with one swipe of its tail, sending them tumbling down a mountain side, where they lay stunned at the bottom. Jesus reared up on his stallion and as its hooves struck the rocky floor, the ground under Satan opened up. Jesus struck him round the face with the flat end of his sword, sending him hurtling down into the huge Abyss that had now opened up. The angels sealed the Abyss so that he could not escape. His cronies, the angels that took his side and were evicted from heaven with him before God created the earth were rounded up and thrown into the Abyss with him. All but one mob of hardened demons were captured. They had occupied the earth and its towns and cities for so long that they knew exactly where to go and hide to avoid being captured. The hunt was on!

ABSINTH, DESPARUS, SLOTH, CULPUS, VIOLENSUS, LUSTUS.

When they saw Jesus coming in the clouds they made a run for freedom and headed to England to one of their favourite hang outs.

Blackpool, Lancashire, England in what remains of the Royal Oak public house. Absinthe, the leader of the renegade mob and his cronies – Desparus, Sloth, Culpus, Violence's and Lustus sit round the open fire near the bar. Culpus feeds wood from broken chairs into the fire to keep it going. They sit around a square bar table, a bottle of Jack Daniels sits in the middle. They drink and talk about the old days.

"I can't believe it's come to this", moans Desparus, sat with his head propped on his scruffy wing, "we were made! We had it all. Now everyone has gone, there's nobody to torment and it's only a matter of time before they come for us". Sloth is sat back in his chair with his legs on the table,

"Will you chill out, just relax we're safe here. They don't know where we are. As long as we keep our heads down we'll be ok". The fire starts to die down and the demons feel the chill of the mid winter air blowing in from over the Irish Sea. Culpus puts more wood onto the fire,

"It's Satan's fault we're in this mess". Violensus springs out of his chair and pins Culpus against the wall of the pub, "Don't talk about our leader like that or I'll...", "Boys, boys relax, have another drink come on!" Absinthe pulls the two squabbling demons apart and with his wings around them both, leads them back to the table and gives them both another shot of JD. "We got to just accept the fact that the good times are over and it's just a matter of time before they come for us. There's nothing we can do about it so just drink and be merry".

"Hey, they were good times too weren't they? How many do you reckon we did over Abs? Ten, fifteen million, since they created liquor"? Absinthe sits back smugly in his chair, his wings behind his head, "I'm not one to boast, but I wreckon about twenty", Absinthe raises his glass, "Here's to team work gentlemen"! The other demons roar with laughter as they raise their glasses, "Teamwork"!!"

"You know that old routine, it never let us down, did it? In 2300 years it worked every time", adds Lustus gloatingly. "Anyone for tennis", Absinthe chips in, the roaring laughter continues, "Doubles of course", "and Violensus and I will jump in at half time" adds Sloth.

"Stupid humans! Most of them just never realised the fun that we were having with them", says Absinthe. "Some of the places we got to hang out in were pretty cool as well, big, posh mansions", adds sloth"and these places were made for us. Hey Violensus, you've thrown many a human through a pub window in your time uuhh!?" laughs Sloth, "Just let me at them! I'll wreck their lives for them"! "Calm down now Violensus its game over now, those days have gone", Absinthe reminds him. "You know Desparus; I got to hand it to you man. You used to wind them up so much during the daylight hours that come 5pm they were begging me to take the pressure off again." "Well I can't take all the credit", replies Desparus, "Culpus you used to torture them something rotten, throwing all that guilt at them, shame on you!", "One aims to please" replies Culpus, the laughter erupts again to the extent that Sloth falls off his chair, "I feel terrible about it now!"

The jokes and laughter continue but elsewhere on earth changes are happening that make it even more essential that Absinthe and his cronies are brought to Justice.

Chapter 3

14 for we believe that Jesus died and rose again, and so we believe, that God will bring with Jesus those who have fallen asleep in him. 15 According to the Lord's word, we tell you that we who are still alive, who are left until the coming of the Lord, will certainly not precede those who have fallen asleep. 16 For the Lord himself will come down from heaven, with a loud command, with the voice of the archangel and with the trumpet call of God, and the dead in Christ will rise first.
1 Thessalonians 4:14-16

St Mary's Church, Manchester. The graveyard looks so quiet early in the morning. There is a white mist hovering over the gravestones. The birds are singing in the trees, somewhat more cheerfully than ever before. Suddenly one of the grave stones falls down. The earth over the grave opens up and its occupier climbs out, brushing himself down he wipes his eyes. Examining himself he notices his new body is bigger, stronger, and more athletic than it ever was before he died. More graves open in the same way. Men and women, some as old as the church step out of their now redundant lodgings to occupy the new earth, God's faithful ones are rising from the dead and not just here, all over the world.

The angels direct the men and women to their new earthly homes. All over the world millions of risen men and women who were faithful to God in their life times are given tasks and responsibilities in the cleanup operation that is now under way.

Their homes are a far cry from what they were used to when they first lived. There are no building, no clothes, no electric or gas. Their bodies are new and super tough. They don't feel the cold. There's no illness or disease any more.

They now live in the forests of the earth, at one with the wild animals, just as their original ancestors Adam and Eve did before the fall.

Those who were carried away into the clouds during the great tribulation return to earth to join their risen ancestors.

Now the process of re-naturalising the earth has begun and every town, village and city has to be returned to its natural state. This has to be done by hand. There's no machinery, no wagons or cars.

The angels have been divided into armies over the whole earth. Their various duties include overseeing the re-naturalisation process, protecting the humans and hunting down the remaining demons that have gone into hiding.

A reconnaissance patrol flying over the Fylde coast picks up heat signals from the North Pier area. The two scouts fly down for a closer look.

They approach the area where the heat signals were coming from and find an old public house; the cinders in the fire are still warm. There is a strong smell of stale alcohol and cigarettes but no sign of life. The scouts record intelligence by scanning the scene and then retreat to headquarters.

Chapter 4

Angel training Camp headquarters, Mount Zion. 0600 hours

The Archangel Michael heads for the training ground where Teetotaller and Justices are training.

Michael watches from the side lines. Teetotaller and Justices hover over the ruins of the ancient village watching for the slightest movement from within the ruins, all is quiet. Suddenly a rogue makes a leap for freedom but Teetotaller pins him with one glance and Justicius makes the arrest. Another rogue flies out of the old bakery and heads for the touchdown located near the side line but Teetotaller flings him into the fountain in the village square with a mere glance, wet and humiliated the rogue steps out of the water and hold his wings up in defeat.

"Nice to see you training hard gentlemen, you're going to need the training because we got an op to carry out and this is a big one", says Michael from the side line. Teetotaller and Justicius look behind them and jump to attention when they see the infamous archangel.

"It must be a big op if they've sent you down Archangel", says Justicius, saluting his superior and straightening his feathers. "What's the job"? "Not here", Michael replies, "1300 hours in the boardroom and I'll debrief you both. Get you tidied up" Michael flies off towards headquarters. The two bounty hunter head for the showers. #changing room scene#

Teetotaller and Justicius walk anxiously down the narrow corridor towards the large boardroom; they are greeted by a host of junior bounty hunters. On entering the room they are greeted by Archangel Michael and introduced to an array of angels who are busy studying holographic intelligence and talking amongst themselves. Michael calls a start to the debriefing and the chattering quickly filters out to complete silence.

"Gentlemen, as you know, since Jesus returned, the cleanup operation is well under way. The angels and God's faithful ones are busy returning the earth to its original beauty and glory. Satan has been locked away in the abyss with many of his cronies for the next thousand years. However, recent intelligence reports have revealed that five of the top ten most wanted demons are hiding away here" a large three dimensional hologram appears in the middle of the boardroom table. "This is what remains of Blackpool in Lancashire, England. Once a hotspot for alcohol and drug abuse. Our angels in the north west of England spotted signs of these demons during a daily patrol of the area – Absinthe, Viol...." "Absinthe"! Shouts Teetotaller, "Just wait until I get my." "Steady on" replies Michael, "I've not finished yet, Absinthe and the rest of his crew - Desparus, Sloth, Culpus, Violensus and Lustus have all been sighted within the last two months in this area of Blackpool". Michael stands up, "Your job gentleman is to capture them and I mean capture them

Teetotaller! No personal vendettas! Bring them in to face a war crimes tribunal."

Michael and Justicius start to discuss the ins and outs of the operation. Teetotaller tries to concentrate but feels himself welling up inside, his mind drifts off, back in time to his previous position in the hosts of angels.......

Guardian Angel Headquarters, level 2, Heavenly Suburbs, 1945

Curatio leaves headquarters to start his days work. He is entrusted with guarding five hundred souls who have asked for a Guardian, he is also entrusted with the souls of two hundred children whose parents have requested a Guardian angel for them. His boss collars him on the way out of the cloud compound.

"Curatio we've just had another request, a young family in Granada have requested a Guardian for their new born, here's the address, fly down and take a look will you", "Yes, general", replies Curatio. Curatio starts his patrol, about mid day he arrives in Granada. He enters the home of the young family and sees the baby in her cot, her mother sat next to her singing nursery rhymes. The mother looks up as Curatio enters the room through the ceiling. She looks round, sensing something; she smiles and continues singing to her baby, Maria. Curatio looks at the mother and child, suddenly a feeling of discomfort comes over him but he can't put his finger on what the problem might be.

"Curatio did you fly by Granada and check out that new born like I asked", "Yes General, I did but there was something I didn't feel comfortable about.

Parents seem fine, home is fine but I got this feeling that something is wrong", reports Curatio,

"Well we don't always know straight away what the problem is, consider it an omen Curatio...watch that one like a hawk...trust your instincts",

"OK, General",

"Any problems you know where I am, keep up the good work",

"Thanks General".

1970

The years go by and Curatio's whim that something is wrong is pushed to the back of his mind as his protégé grows up, attends school, college and then gets married herself. He's acted on a few occasions, like the time she nearly fell in a swimming pool and another time when she wasn't paying attention crossing the road, he was there to pull her back to safety.

Maria started to feel stressed and anxious after the birth of her first child. She was struggling to adapt to being a mother. Drinking was very much a part of Spanish culture and Maria really enjoyed a couple of glasses of red wine at lunch time. Over time she started to look forward to her lunch time drink. By the time her baby was two years old the lunch time drinking had crept forward a couple of hours and Maria was having a glass or two at breakfast. Her husband began to feel concerned about this as by 3pm she was a bit wobbly. One afternoon Maria had had a lot to drink, it was about 5pm. She was driving to the supermarket to get some shopping.

Curatio was in France at the time when the old feeling that something was not right with Maria suddenly re-emerged and he knew he had to get to her straight away.

Maria was driving the car down the inside lane of the dual carriage way. Her baby was strapped in the back of the car. The baby was crying because Maria had put the harness on too tight. Maria could barely concentrate on the road she had drunk that much, she was veering from one lane to another. The passing cars blasted their horns and signalled to her to get off the road. She turned round to check on her child and the car veered onto the wrong side of the carriage way, an oncoming lorry driver saw Maria's car heading straight for him, he hit the brakes hard but it was raining and the road was slippery. Curatio got there in the nick of time and kicked Maria's car off the road into a ditch. The lorry came to a halt to see what had happened to Maria. Dazed but unhurt she looked behind her to see her baby safe in the back. She noticed that the front of her car was mangled. She undid the seat belt and took her baby out of the car. Within minutes the police arrived and breathalysed Maria. She was arrested and her baby was taken off her until her husband could get to the station. Curatio had saved her life but he could not interfere with the consequences of her own actions.

Losing her licence and getting a criminal record for drink driving led Maria into despair. Her family were disappointed with her. Her husband was angry because he had to stop working full time and work part time now to drive them round. Maria felt guilty about what she had done but the worse she felt during the day, the more she felt the need to reach for a drink.

One day shortly after the accident there was a knock at the door. Maria staggered to the door and two women barged in to her home. One of the women showed Maria her identification. "
Andrea Fay, Social Services. We believe you had a car accident Mrs Escobar and you were found to be drunk in charge of a motor vehicle and also in charge of a minor?"
"Yes but I'm ok now." Maria staggers back into the lounge and the two social workers see the child playing on the floor. Fays eyes light up when she sees the child, "Brownie points!" she thinks to herself.
"You've been drinking today haven't you Mrs Escobar, I can smell it on your breath!"
"I'm fine!"
"Your drunk in charge of a minor, we can't leave you here with the baby. We'll have to take her."
Maria dashes towards her child to pick him up but the other social worker grabs the baby and dashes towards the front door. A struggle breaks out between Maria and Fay but the police come in and arrest Maria and take her to the police station.
Her distraught husband goes to the police station and bails his wife. The distraught couple ask the police to give them their child back but they are told to call children's services in the morning. The couple return home in despair, broken hearted and upset.
The morning after Pedro calls his solicitor and he calls children's services

immediately. They are told that the child is to remain in care as he is at risk of being neglected. Maria has to agree to go to counselling until she has given up drinking, unless her husband gives up his job and stay at home all day. Eventually after a three month court case the couple agree that Pedro will only work part-time and his mother will look after the baby at home with Maria until she has stopped drinking. The pair had a lucky escape and Fay was not happy.

1988

Pedro spent the next sixteen years covering up for Maria, to protect them from social services and nosy school teachers who were always concerned about their child's welfare. He became an expert at covering things up and giving everybody the impression that everything was alright at home, when in reality it wasn't, he was miserable, but good at holding things together. There were sporadic good times but after sixteen years they had grown apart so much and Pedro knew that there was nothing left in their marriage. He got the child to school and did his best to keep the house clean and tidy himself.

When his son was about fourteen he became good friend with someone from school. One night his friend got into a bit of trouble and Pedro ended up having to go round to their house to see what was going on. He only popped round to make sure everything was alright. Francisco's mum lived on her own, she had three kids and she had her own problems. Pedro was speechless when he met her for the first time. She was beautiful. Their house was clean and tidy and there was a real bond of friendship between them right from the start which over time got stronger and stronger. Pedro started to help her sort her life out and she became a really good and loyal friend to him.

Maria's husband had had enough. The binge drinking, the debts, the arguments. He packed a suitcase and told Maria that he was going to live on his own because he couldn't stand to see what she was doing to herself any longer. Maria's son chose to go with his dad, leaving Maria on her own. Maria begged her husband not to go. In a final attempt to get him to stay she lost it, picked up a glass ashtray and hurled it at him. The missile barely missed his head.

"That's it Maria, that's the final straw, your drinking has led you to violence, it's over".

Curatio observed from above. He wept as he saw Maria destroying herself and he knew that he could not interfere with her own choices. He was helpless to intervene.

1998

A dishevelled skinny woman staggers down the side streets of Granada's student quarter bumping into everybody she passes. Her clothes stink. She has a bottle of Absinthe in her right hand and a cigarette in the other. She begs some passing tourists to give her some money but they cross over to the other side of the street. She turns down a back alley, as she stands there alone she sees six shadows surrounding her, she hears their voices taunting her,

"It's your entire fault Maria!"

"What have you done to yourself?"

"Screw the lot of them Maria, just have another drink!"

As she stands there in despair, tears pouring down her eyes, she turns round to see a dark shadow standing over her. The force of the push sends her hurtling to the ground. She hits her head on the curb stone, blood pouring from her face she lies there, unable to move or cry out for help, her eyes close for the last time.

Curatio cries out in agony at losing a soul. He sees them leaving the scene and makes a b line for Absinthe. The others attack him as Curatio grabs Absinthe by the throat and pins him against a wall, but he sends them hurtling back down the alley with his wing. Curatio is just about to leather Absinthe when he is taken away from the scene and wakes up back at headquarters.

Curatio's cell is small and grey. There's a bed and a toilet in the small grotty room that he wakes up in. He gathers his thoughts trying to remember what happened to Absinthe and his cronies.

A guard comes in and ushers Curatio down a long corridor into an interview room. He is greeted by Archangel Michael.

"Curatio, do you remember what you did and why we had to physically extract you from that situation"?

Curatio says nothing, he remembers what happened,

"They killed her! They taunted her from the day her child was born and then they murdered her in that dark alley Michael"!

"Be that as it may Curatio, you are an angel and you can not react out of vengeance, if you do you are just as bad as them..........you were going to be court marshalled for your behaviour but you've been granted a pardon from Jesus himself",

Curatio looks startled,

"God has seen your pain at loosing Maria. From now on Curatio you will be known as Teetotaller. You are to spend the next forty years at Bounty Hunter Training School preparing for your new role. Don't see this as a promotion though, consider it a side step. You've had a lucky escape and it has gone down on your record."

"Tee! Tee! Are you still with us? Wake up for goodness sake will you", shouts Archangel Michael, standing at the head of the boardroom table.

Justicius looks shocked at Teetotaller and whispers "Get a grip will you!"

"Yes, Sir, Archangel" Tee sits up straight.

"The operation will commence at 0500 hours next Thursday gentlemen; you'll be accompanied by a team of junior bounty hunters from the Cheshire regiment. You've got a week to finish training, make the most of it"!

Archangel Michael looks disapprovingly at Teetotaller and leaves the room, he seems agitated.

Chapter 5

0300 On the day of the Round Up operation. Justicius and Teetotaller finish breakfast and make their way to the exit of the training camp. Michael is already there waiting for them.

"A word with you Tee, if I may", Michael takes Teetotaller to one side.

"Good look today Tee. Remember your job is to bring them in alive. It's not our place to judge. God alone has that privilege. Can you put your strong feelings aside? I don't want you messing this operation up"!

"I can archangel and I will", replies Tee,

"OK, get on with it then and God bless you all!"

Tee and Justicius roar out of the training camp headed towards Blackpool. They rendezvous with the junior bounty hunters at 0430 hours in Southport.

Absinthe and his cronies are still asleep. The sun is just coming up over Blackpool. Lustus comes round slowly as daylight starts to come through the pub windows. Justicius and Tee lead the Bounty Hunters to the perimeter of the pub and surround it completely. Absinthe starts to stir. He opens his eyes and stands up, stretching his wings.

"Sloth get up you lazy oaf. Get some breakfast on come on!"

"Get stuffed, you do it!" replies sloth.

"Desparus, get some breakfast on will you!"

Desparus puts the old frying pan on the remains of last night's fire and gets some bacon, sausage and eggs out of the back kitchen. He bundles it all into the frying pan and sits cooking the food whilst smoking his first cigarette of the day. Lustus and Culpus start to stir now as the smell of full English starts to fill the room. Metus gets up and has a pee against the curtains at the back of the pub.

"Metus you dirty sod how many time have I told you not to do that!" Shouts Absinthe, but Metus doesn't hear him.

"What now"?! He replies. Suddenly the doors burst open as the bounty hunters storm the pub. Two of the juniors capture Sloth and cuff him, "You're nicked fatty"! "Bog off", retorts Sloth. Two more juniors make a run at Absinthe but Violensus sees them coming and hurls them through the pub window. Tee flies at Violensus and throws him into the fire. His wings go up in flames as he writhes around on the floor trying to put the fire out. Two of the juniors cuff him and take him away. Absinthe picks up a bar stool and launches it at Tee. The stool catches him on the chest and sends him hurtling across the bar. He picks himself up of the floor and launches himself full throttle at Absinthe. He pins him down on the floor.

"Here we are again eh Tee, or is it Curatio? How's Maria?" laughs Absinthe, "You're nicked Absinthe; hope you like it hot because it's sure hot where you're going"! Absinthe manages to break free and flies off out of the window. He heads for the remains of Blackpool tower and hides in the ballroom right at the very top. Teetotaller is fresh on his tail and follows him into the old circus. Inside its dark and gloomy. Teetotaller searches for Absinthe but can't find him anywhere. Suddenly Absinthe jumps out from behind the curtains and flies at Te. They both tumble down the gangway between the isles of old seats. They both grab prop swords that have been discarded on the floor of the theatre and a mighty battle begins between the two of them. Absinthe attacks Te fearlessly as they fight in mid air. Te picks up a full row of chairs and hurls it at Absinthe it lands on top of him. He lies there motionless and Te stands over him and cuffs his wings so he can't fly off. Then the guardians come and take him away. The other bounty hunters capture Lustus and Desparus. Justicius make a run at Culpus but he pulls out an old gun that had been left under the bar and shoots him in the stomach. Justicius falls to the ground clutching his stomach. Culpus takes a pop shot at Tee but he ducks and grabs a handful of smouldering cinders out of the fire and throws them into Culpus's face. He kicks him between the legs and cuffs him.

"Game over Culpus"!

Culpus scream in agony, his face charred and inflamed.

The junior bounty hunters take them all in. Justicius stands up clutching his stomach,

"Are you alright"? Asks Tee,

"Yes, it just winded me that's all". Justicius and Tee make their way back to headquarters.

Chapter 5

Jerusalem, the angels and God's faithful were busy clearing away the debris of the old earth ready for the New Jerusalem that would descend from heaven at the right time.

Hosts of angels, some ten to twenty thousand per platoon worked together clearing the ground in preparation for its arrival. The size of the city would be 2200km square. The land underneath and around the city had to be cleared of all buildings, concrete, graves, as nothing impure would ever be allowed to enter the city.

It was now becoming increasingly important to ensure that the remaining demons were tried and imprisoned in the abyss with Satan, as the arrival of the New Jerusalem was being delayed by them now. The following decree had already been issued to the angels -

'Nothing impure will ever enter it, nor will anyone who does what is shameful or deceitful, but only those whose names are written in the Lamb's book of life' Rev 21:27

Alcatraz Island, San Francisco, USA.

The resurrected prison was a hive of activity now. The whole island was surrounded by angels due to its new guests.

Absinthe, Sloth, Lustus, Violensus, Desparus and Culpus were now safely locked away behind bars.

The inner rooms of the prison were now a hive of activity as lawyers and court officials prepared for the impending trial. The district attorney preparing the case for the prosecution was Helga Petrova, a Russian American lawyer who, during her forty year career, had worked her way up to District Attorney of Washington. As a devoted follower she survived Armageddon and was whisked away with the rest of God's faithful ones. On her return she was ushered here to be debriefed by the angel Gabriel.

Petrova sits waiting for Gabriel, she's ushered in by an angel, and Gabriel greets her,

"Helga, nice to meet you, come in. I imagine you've no idea why you've been brought here, or why there's even a case to prepare"? Petrova looks up at Gabriel and can't believe that she's actually talking to an angel, let alone been chosen to prepare a case for him.

"Relax Helga, yes the wings are real" Helga bows to Gabriel and starts to talk but Gabriel interrupts,

"Hey don't bow to me please; I'm just a servant of the Lord just like you. Have you forgotten that you humans are actually ranked higher than the angels"?

"Sorry" replies Petrova nervously, "So what are we doing here"?

"Do you recognise these guys"? Gabriel shows Helga the mug shots of Absinthe and his cronies,

"They've just been brought in and locked away here at Alcatraz. We can't just throw them into the abyss with Satan and the rest of his crew. Absinthe is demanding a lawyer. He won't talk. He wreckons he's never laid a finger on anyone and claims that his victims chose to drink themselves to death. "Free Will!" This poses a big dilemma for us Helga because as you know, we can't act against free will. If Absinthe's lawyer can prove that his victims chose to drink themselves to death then he and cronies could walk out of here free spirits and delay the creation of the new heaven. Then God's going to be a bit annoyed! Do you see now why this case is so important"?

"What evidence do we have to start building a case with"? asks Petrova, "and what have they allegedly done that's so bad that it warrants a war crime tribunal"?

"World war two saw 60 million souls lost to war. The world health organisation has evidence to prove that before the return of Jesus, Absinthe and his cronies were responsible for, are you ready for this"?,

'2.5 Million Alcohol-Related Deaths Worldwide- Annually'

Gabriel continues,

"Saddam Hussein's total death toll was less than 1% of what this son of a .... was doing annually"

"Do we know how he operates and can we prove it"? Asks Petrova,

"This is where you come in Petrova. We have to build a case against Absinthe and his mob, the rest of them - Sloth, Lustus, Violensus, Desparus and Culpus, pictured here, they worked as team, taunting their victims."

"Have they been charged yet? We can't hold them forever if they've not been charged"!

"That our next job", replies Gabriel.

Petrova makes her way in through the labyrinth of prison corridors, accompanied by four guardians. As they reach the high security, solitary confinement block she becomes aware at just how high security this part of the prison is. She feels nervous. Before they are allowed to enter Absinthe's cell Petrova is ushered into a doctor's room. The doctor asks Petrova,

"Have you ever had a problem with alcohol Miss Petrova"?

"No, never", she replies, the doctor examines her for signs of alcohol related illnesses.

"His cell is divided into two to protect you from him. His eyes are covered so that he can't look you in the eyes. Eye contact is all he needs to tempt you. Don't tell him anything about yourself. If you do he will find a way into your mind. Don't show any signs of weakness whatsoever."

"Ok doctor" replies Petrova,

"You're feeling nervous aren't you? You can't go in like that he'll sense it! Have you forgotten who you're working for Helga? The lord himself has chosen you for this job. Go in there in His name, not in any strength of your own".

Petrova suddenly feels better; she feels that the lord is with her. She stands up straight, confident,

"Let's do this! She leaves the doctors room and prepares to enter Absinthe's cell with the guardians.

The prison guard slowly starts to unlock the prison cell door. He glances at Petrova uncomfortably as she enters the cell. Absinthe is stood there separated from her by iron bars. His eyes are covered and his wings are secured with thick chains so that he can't move around or attempt to escape.

Petrova sits at the square table set back from the bars of the prison cell. She slowly opens her file and addresses Absinthe,

"I gather you know why you are here"?

There is silence, he doesn't reply to her question.

"You can't stay quiet forever Absinthe…"

"I want to speak to my lawyer" he replies,

"You got nothing on me, nothing. I'm an entertainer that's all, you can't prove anything"

"Absinthe you are hereby charged with genocide and will remain in custody to face a war crimes tribunal".

"Bring it on bitch! Hey I knew your grandmother back in mother Russia. Me and her we go back a long way you know! Ha ha ha",

Petrova remembered vaguely the stories of how her grandmother died falling down the stairs, drunk out of her head.

"Get me out of here" Petrova snapped at the guard,

"I'll see you in court!"

"Whatever hey don't forget my lawyer"!

Petrova storms out of the cell, tears running down her face, shocked at the intrusion into her personal family past and now intensely aware of how dangerous this demon really is.

Petrova returns to Gabriel's office. She stops by the prison chapel on her way to compose herself. As she sits there Gabriel comes in and sits next to her,

"He got to you didn't he?" asks Gabriel tenderly,

"Just for a minute. I charged him anyway and now he's demanding a lawyer."

"His lawyer is on his way as we speak. Take some time now to compose yourself and when you're ready I'll introduce you to the investigator who is going to lead this case. OK?"

Gabriel slowly leaves the chapel.

Chapter 6

John Smith was a latecomer into God's flock. A defence lawyer with thirty years experience at defending some of the world's most notorious criminals. He came to Christ through a preacher that he represented in the end times who had been convicted of promoting Christianity after the world wide ban in 2040.

Even though John lost the case and the elderly preacher was sentenced to death, John sensed that the preacher was a good man at heart, probably the only genuine, good natured man he had ever defended in thirty years.

As the preacher sat on death row waiting for his own execution John visited him for the last time.

"Hi Reverend, I hope you don't mind me coming to visit you",

"Not at all", replied the elderly preacher, "Please come in, you are welcome".

"I came to say how sorry I am that things have turned out this way for you",

"John you need not apologise my friend. I am and always have been prepared to die for my faith. The tribulation we are in now is no surprise to any of us; in fact it's an omen that Satan's reign on earth is nearly over. John!

don't miss the boat my friend. Make your choices very carefully because time is running out for you to decide whose side you are batting for. Read the good book and decide for yourself my friend.

John smiled, "

"You don't give up do you; you are totally devoted to your God, even now, four hours before your execution"

"Absolutely", replied the old preacher with a tear in his eye.

"I'm proud to die for him. A little apprehensive I guess as well!" the two men chuckle at the preacher's ominous predicament.

The cell door opens and two guards enter,

"Times up Mr Smith, the preacher has got be processed before the execution".

John stands up and looks the preacher in the eyes,

"Goodbye Reverend",

"Let's just say adieu. I've got a hunch that we will meet again John. Remember make your choices very carefully John. Time is running out".

The youngest of the guards gets impatient and grabs the elderly preacher by the arm and drags him to his feet,

"Come on you mad old fool, there's nothing he can do for you now, get a move on", John intervenes, "Hey! Is it too much trouble to treat an elderly man with a bit of respect in his final hour"? The other guard directs John out of the cell forcefully, "Your time's up buddy, on your way. You wouldn't want to give anyone the impression that you're siding with this old fool would you? Move on now!"

John leaves the cell and walks with his head down towards the exit. He feels a choking sense of loss and finality, yet a sense of hope and freedom that seems too scary to acknowledge because it would be to do the unthinkable. To acknowledge Christ as Saviour is an immediate death sentence in this day and age.

As the final years went by after the preacher's execution John did read the good book and made his commitment to Christ in 2047.

He was debarred, arrested and thrown into prison. Sat in his own cell now he felt for the first time how it feels to be on the wrong side of the bars.

Two days before he was due in court for sentencing he was being transported from prison to the Courts of Justice. The old yellow prison bus sped down the highway en route to Washington DC. John had defended several of the other prisoners that were there with him on the bus. Suddenly John and three of the other inmates on the bus found themselves flying through the air up towards the clouds. The sky was literally full of people floating upwards. Back on earth cars and buses crashed as drivers were literally whisked away leaving speeding vehicles vacant, many of them now unmanned missiles headed for the unbelievers who had been left behind. Turmoil erupted on earth as a large chunk of the earth's population just disappeared into the clouds.

Chapter 7

The Investigation

John Smith was back. He arrived back on earth along with the other believers. He was impressed by his new body. He'd always had a bad leg since he was eight years old and was hit by a car coming out of school. His new legs were big, strong and perfect in every way. He liked the idea that now there was no such thing as pain. It just wasn't in the dictionary any more.

He wasn't over the moon at being ordered to represent Absinthe. He'd been hoping that his job in the new kingdom would be better than representing more dumb criminals but he kept quiet and obedient. The up side of it all was that Absinthe was a renowned mob leader of the demon kingdom. If he was successful in defending him it would look good on his CV. Not a bad way to finish a career bearing in mind that this would be his last case. Now that all the unbelievers had gone there was no need for lawyers any more.

John made his way to Absinthe's cell accompanied by two guards. He went through the same process that the DA Helga had been though, questioned by the doctor about his drinking habits. He entered Absinthe's cell and sat at the table opposite the bars.

"About time!" Were Absinthe's first words to John? "Where are my friends?"

"They're all locked up Absinthe. You've been charged with genocide by poisoning, using the toxic substance alcohol. How do you intend to plead at the moment?"

"Absolutely not guilty. John they chose to shovel the liquor down their own throats. I'm an entertainer you know, that's all. They got depressed, anxious, and downhearted. I cheered them up. I want bail John. Can you get us out of here?"

"I'll put in a request for bail as soon as I can just bear with me. There's going be a lengthy investigation Abs. You've taken everyone by surprise as nobody was expecting you to deny the charges".

Courts of Justice. Washington.

There's a hive of activity in the outer offices of the Courts of Justice. Edginess has spread through the entire kingdom at the news that Absinthe has requested a defence and is pleading not guilty. The news has spread so fast that even Jesus himself has heard about it and has expressed concerns that a lengthy trial would delay the opening of the new heavenly city. If his lawyer is that good what will happen if he gets off? Can his lawyer prove free will?

Petrova and Gabriel sit waiting for the investigator whose been chosen to support the prosecution for this case. Dr Alex floss a time served psychological profiler for the FBI has been brought in to lead the investigation. Before the believers were whisked away Floss worked on many famous cases, mostly profiling serial killers and terrorist leaders.

Floss arrives with his team of investigators.

"Dr Floss, can we get straight down to work please, time is of the essence", Petrova and Gabriel usher Floss and his team over to the hub of the investigation room.

"We suspect that Absinthe and his cronies worked as a team. They thought they were untouchable",

"What evidence do we have to begin with, to launch an investigation?" ask Floss,

"There are over 70 million souls Dr Floss that departed this earth due to Absinthe and his crew and time is of the essence in creating a case against them", Gabriel replies. "Here you can access the database of souls that we hold at present"

Floss and his team get to work siphoning their way through the millions of death certificates linked to Absinthe and his cronies.

Floss profiles Absinthe.

Records indicate that Absinthe was first seen in or around 10 000 BC during the Neolithic period. Then in ancient Egypt he managed to set himself up as a local 'God' known as Osiris – the god of wine.

Not unlike Heroinas, Cocainas, Lustus and a few other high profile demons of that era Absinthe played on the void in a human's soul that was there from birth caused by mankind's separation from God in Eden.

This void caused inexplicable cravings in mankind and caused them to spend their lives chasing after all sorts of things from bling to mind altering substances. Like tourists on a bus with the curtains closed they never stopped to enjoy the present, they just kept on living in the future, looking for the next thing that might fill that awful empty void in their souls.

One of his first recruits was in India. A Forrester called Zura noticed some birds asleep under a tree. He examined the tree and noticed that a there was liquid in a pool that had been created by a branch snapping off during a storm. The birds deposited rice and other fruits in to the little pool and over time the sun heated the water up. He tasted the liquid and felt like dancing and singing so then he introduced his friend Barruna to the liquid and encouraged him to drink this instead of meditating. Zura and Barruna hoped they could make money selling this liquid so they start by offering some to the king. The king liked it and they started to create it synthetically but the more everybody drank the less inclined they were to work. In the end the king went bankrupt so the pair moved on to another kingdom.

Over the centuries Absinthe carried on recruiting salesmen who would market his product. In 1000 AD he clenched his first major business deal with Vladimir The Great, in Russia, who rejected Islam as a state religion for the country due to its prohibition of alcohol. Ivan the Terrible took this one step further by creating taverns throughout Russia and Absinthe and his cronies were now well on their way to being 'made men' the government were raking it in from Absinthe's products and their fame and success was spreading worldwide. Deaths between 1990 and 2001 of residents in three Siberian industrial towns determined that 52% of deaths of people between the ages of 15 and 54 were the result of Absinthe and his crew.

In America attempts to ban alcohol opened more doors for Absinthe and his cronies as organized crime received a major boost from Prohibition. Absinthe introduced Lustus to his crew and prostitution, gambling, and theft were big business until 1920, when organized smuggling or 'bootlegging' started in response to the effect of Prohibition. A profitable, often violent, black market for alcohol emerged. Absinthe created powerful criminal gangs and corrupted law enforcement agencies, which lead to racketeering. Consequently, prohibition provided Absinthe and his cronies with a financial market for organized crime to flourish.

Rather than reducing crime it seemed Prohibition had made the cities into battlegrounds between opposing bootlegging gangs. The Volstead Act which had been created to reduce the harm caused by Absinthe led to worse social conditions than before the prohibition, as shown by more lethal forms of alcohol, an increase in crime rates, and the creation of a black market dominated by criminal organizations. Abs and his crew were going from strength to strength.

In 17th Century Great Britain Absinthe's creation of pubs and taverns was a raging success. Desparus cashed in on the poverty of the day by frequenting work houses were poor despairing people went to die.

Absinthe initiated the Gin Craze. A period in the first half of the 18th century when the consumption of Gin increased enormously in Great Britain, especially in London. Many people drank too much and the city had an epidemic of extreme drunkenness; this caused a real outrage in the country but Absinthe was laughing and his cronies were busier than ever before, destroying the lives of people who just couldn't see what was happening to them because they were so subtle and expert in their team work.

Famous people were easy targets for Abs and his crew as the stress of public life took its toll. They accrued a record hit list of some 61 famous people from silent film actress Julia Bruns in 1927 to Singer Any Winehouse in 2011.

Back in the USA Absinthe teamed up with Jack Danyal amongst other affluent distillers from around the world such as Abraham Ball in Scotland.

Adolph Mush in Germany / America. From their initiation into Absinthe's lucrative corporate world to the return of Jesus' these companies went from strength to strength. In the 90s and noughties Alco pops rose to tremendous popularity. The numbers of young people with alcohol related illnesses rose alarmingly in the end times.

Seven days later, the team are still working diligently through the records they hold. Caroline Sparrow, Floss's deputy investigator looks excited as she sits at her desk. Floss stands behind her as she sits working,

"What have you come up with Sparrow? I know that look in your eye",

"I've found at least six local records linked to Absinthe and his crew. Five of them have risen. Three are in the abyss but they have family that have risen and are working on the naturalisation plains nearby",

"Good work Sparrow. Locate them and let's go and talk to them. We need a concrete case based on a small number of victims."

Sparrow makes her way to the naturalisation plant in Seattle. Her first victim Helen Brown is busy bagging grass seed on a large production line for the angels to use.

"Helen, my name name's Agent Sparrow FBI, could we have a chat for a minute please?"

"Sure", Helen leaves the production line and leads Sparrow to a quiet clearing in the forest. They sit on a log and Sparrow starts the interview.

Sparrow shows Helen the mug shots of Absinthe and his cronies.

"We've seen your death certificate Helen and wondered if you recognise any of these guys?"

Helen looks carefully at the photos and a look of fear comes over her.

"It's ok Helen. They can't hurt you now they are all locked up behind bars". Swallow reassures her.

"I met this one here for the first time when I was about seventeen. He called himself something different back then...Jack...Jack....Daniels that's it. Boy he was funny, kept me entertained for hours. I didn't like his friends though. As the years went by and I got to know his friends", Helen bursts into tears,

"It's ok Helen go on?"

"This fat one here..."

"Sloth"

"Yes, that's him. After a night with Absinthe, sloth used to come and tell me not to go to work. He used to get quite pushy, Said I should stay home",

"Did he force you to stay home or did you choose to stay home?" asked Swallow,

"He didn't force me but this guy here Desparus. He was a bad egg. I never liked him from the start. As soon as I woke up after a night with Abs, Desparus was there taunting me, he made me feel too depressed to go to work so in the end it was easier to just give into to Sloth and stay home."

"Then what would happen?" asked Swallow,

"This guy here Culpus. He would drop by usually around mid day or just after work had phoned me to ask me why I wasn't in. He used to bully me, push me around. He told me that all the shit in my life was my fault and that I was a bad person."

"Did you believe him?"

"Most times."

"What about this guy Violensus?"

"I never met him but there was another one... Metus. He was a nasty son of a...he used to come round with Desparus. He terrified me most of the time. Made me feel like I was going to die."

"So Desparus and Metus would taunt you all day?"

"Yes until Abs got back anyway, usually around three or four in the afternoon. Abs used to send them on their way. He would see me so upset and put his arms around me, make me feel special and confident you know.

"It says on your death certificate that you were found dead in you flat. You'd taken some pain killers?"

My child had just been taken into care at the time. I'd fought long and hard to keep her but the social workers just came up with lie upon lie to soil my case. I'd take ten steps forward and they would twist it to make that look like ten steps backwards."

"Can you prove in any way that the social workers were in cahoots with Desparus and the rest of them?"

"Yes, look," Helen shows Swallow a pile of court papers, "on the final day of the hearing my litigation friend had to submit a statement about how I felt and he had asked an educated friend of his to look at all the court papers. This friend picked out about thirty flaws in the social service's case against me that were either untrue or over exaggerated. When I took it to my lawyer he went berserk. He refused to use it and said that my litigation friend would be in trouble for submitting this. In trouble for pointing out the truth! Can you believe that?"

"What kind of discrepancies were there?

"They were supposed to come and check my home to ensure that it was suitable for a child to come out of foster care. They gave me 24 hours notice to come and check my home. I'd told them that I had builders in at the time but they still came and based their assessment on what the house was like with builders making a mess. They did not put it in their report that I had builders in at the time, just that the property was unsuitable. After losing her I started drinking again."

"Desparus, Culpus and Metus were round at mine again. Absinthe was there as well but he had stopped defending me, just kept telling me to drink more. He had changed. He kept demanding that I drink so much before he would show me any affection. Sloth had cost me my job and my child. They just rang me one day and said don't come in again. Culpus really laid into me about that but it was Sloth who told me to stay home and Metus who told me that I'd get fired going into work in that state. In the end they cost me my job anyway."

"And the night you died?" asked Sparrow almost impatiently,

"I was only thirty at the time. They would not let up; they kept hounding me night and day. I don't remember too much about that night. I'd fallen over in the path and hurt my back, I could hardly walk. Another friend of theirs came by and I'd never met this guy before."

"What did he say to you Helen?"

"He told me to just take some pain killers with a glass of JD and I'd feel much better. Abs agreed, said it would stop my back ache. The last thing I remember is taking those pain killers. The next thing I'm clawing my way out of a grave in the pouring rain."

"Helen I really need to know who this other demon was, do you recall what they called him?"

"He, she was called Su."

"Do you believe that what happened to you was your fault Helen?"

"They taunted and bullied me. Abs was great to begin with but towards the end he was so demanding. I should never have got mixed up with them in the first place".

"Helen will you testify in court. Stand up and tell a jury what you have told me today?"

"I will"

Sparrow reports back to Floss. Floss is pleased that they have their first concrete witness.

"There are these other guys Su and Metus. Have you any idea who they are Dr Floss?

"Oh I think I have an idea. Leave that one with me Sparrow. Where are you headed to next?

"Spain, Granada. There's a guy there whose wife was found dead down an alleyway. She's not risen but he is and he has come forward himself to give evidence."

"Good work sparrow keep me posted. I'm going to pay a visit to the abyss."

The abyss is now a high security prison. It's surrounded by God's hardest angels and the top of it is covered with a 6 metre thick metal grid than spans the whole of its surface.

Floss approaches the Archangel in charge of the abyss and requests that Metus and Su be brought out for questioning and to face trial.

"On whose authority am I supposed to let these prisoners go Dr Floss?"

"I have this warrant for their arrest", the archangel looks at the warrant, "Issued by the district attorney" adds Floss. The stench of Burning flesh is too much for Floss and he cruckles, clutching his stomach in one hand and covering his nose with the other. The archangel takes pity on him and orders the two demons to be brought up quickly.

"They're on their way up to you Dr Floss, you get out of here sir! This is no place for a believer.

The two demons are taken back to Alcatraz with the rest of the mob.

The angel Navigator descends into Granada. Sparrow holds on nervously. She was never keen on aeroplanes let alone riding on an angel's back. The navigator lands safely at the home of Pedro Escobar. The man who came forward himself to give evidence against the demons.

Sparrow knocks on the door of Pedro's home. Mr Escobar answers the door and usher sparrow into the lounge.

"Sit down please Miss Sparrow. Can I get anything to drink?"

"Fresh orange if you have some please". Sparrow sits and waits in the little lounge as Pedro prepares her drink.

"This is a lovely little house Mr Escobar!"

"I'm lucky to still have it. Naturalisation is due to start here in a couple of months. This part of Granada is very quiet and mainly unspoilt by the old world order; hence the angels haven't deemed the city a high priority as yet."

"I'm sure our new homes will be more splendid than anything we've ever conceived of" assures sparrow.

"I'm sure…so you want to know about Absinthe Miss Sparrow?"

"Yes, can you tell me what you know? Where you affected yourself or did you lose a loved one?"

"I lost my wife to Absinthe and his cronies. Maria's drinking started when our son was born. Over the years it got worse and worse. By the time our son was eighteen I'd had enough. We both left. The last time I saw her she threw an ash tray at me, nearly took my head off. I'm told that she was found dead in an alleyway in the student quarter a couple of miles from here. She was deceived by Absinthe all our married life and beyond. She looked terrible throughout the mornings and never chirped up until she'd had her first drink. Towards the end of our marriage there was no break in her drinking. The minute she woke up she would be drinking again. "

Swallow showed Pedro the mug shots of Absinthe's cronies.

"Do you recognise any of these guys"? Asked Swallow,

"Yes, all of them, Desparus and Sloth were always around in the morning. She gave up caring about our home; she just sat feeling sorry for herself most of the time. Culpus was a regular visitor as well; he used to show up with Metus. They taunted her something rotten and that son of bitch Absinthe would simply hold out his arms and comfort Maria, even though towards the end he would make her drink so much before he would do anything for her. Pedro sat with his hands over his face; tears welled up in his eyes.

"I'm sorry Mr Escobar; I imagine this must be really painful for you to talk about."

"He sighs deeply. The pain of knowing that she did not return with the believers is bad enough. She never made a commitment. The way she died in that dirty back street is tragic.so tragic."

"Is there anything else that you can tell me, anything that might lead us to more evidence about how Maria was taunted by these demons?"

"No not really......there was something strange that happened at the funeral. Maria's mother was quite old by the time Maria died. She felt that her prayer had gone unanswered, attending the funeral of her own daughter. It knocked her faith a bit."

"What prayer was that Mr Escobar?"

"A prayer for a Guardian Angel. When Maria was born her mother prayed a Guardian Angel over her new born."

"Interesting…I'll follow that up, thank you for your time Mr Escobar"

"Don't mention it. If you need me to testify just let me know where and when."

"We will thank you!"

Sparrow gets back in contact with Floss at Alcatraz.

"Hi boss, an interesting development here. Can you ask Gabriel to find out about Maria Escobar? See if she was ever assigned a Guardian angel. It seems her mother requested one for her when she was born but mother was left feeling that her prayer went unanswered."

"I don't think that's possible. I'll look into it and get back to you. I'm just about to go and interview Su. They've just arrived here from the abyss. If Maria did have a Guardian he will probably be able to shed some light on how she died"

Floss Interviews Su.

Floss sits in a grotty cold interview room with Petrova, the DA, in the upper rooms of Alcatraz. Su is brought in and handcuffed to his chair. He is blindfolded so that he can't look floss and Petrova in the eyes.

"What am I doing here? Who are you?"

"My name's Dr Alex Floss, FBI. This is the DA Helga Petrova. Su we want to know about your involvement in the death of Helen Brown. Where you there that night when she died?"

"I ain't telling you jack shi…"

"If you think it's hot on the upper levels of the abyss Su imagine how bad it would be if you got sent down further. It can be arranged! now spill the beans and I'll see about getting you elevated a bit nearer the surface!"

"How do I know that you're not just saying that?"

"You don't...but a thousand years is a long time. If we get a conviction in this case, you! Absinthe and the rest of his mob are going straight to the lowest level for the duration. One thousand years, twelve thousand months Su!"

"OK ok, what do you want to know and how far up will I get for this disclosure?!"

"Were you there that night when she died?"

"I believe I called in. She was in a bad way, bent double. She'd fallen over on the path outside. Metus and Desparus were busting her balls and Abs was refusing to make her feel better unless she drank more."

"What did you say to her Su?"

"I didn't like to see her in pain you know! I suggested that a couple of pain killers with a glass of JD would simply ease the pain. A kind gesture I thought"

Petrova bangs her open hand down angrily on the desk,

"It didn't cross your mind that the alcohol in her blood mixed with paracetamol would kill her!? Don't take the piss Su! Or is it Suicidus, full name! We know all about you Suicidus. The reason you were in the abyss in the first place is because of your involvement with Desparus and the millions that took their own lives. Now you're even deeper up to your neck in it!" Petrova shouts angrily.

Su starts to look a little worried, wondering if he's already said too much.

"What else do you want to know? Let's plea bargain!"

"Tell us about the whole mob Su. How did they operate? asks Dr Floss,

"Hey if I tell you that, I want to be well away from the rest of them guys back in the abyss. I want protection."

"Tell us what you know Su and you'll get protection", adds the DA.

"OK...............they're a racket. Abs always starts the ball rolling. You know what a smooth talker he is. He kept them smiling, gave them confidence. One he got them hooked he wanted to keep them hooked so Desparus would then join the game. He gave them a reason to need Absinthe – freedom from the despair. Metus and Culpus they just backed up Desparus. Violensus, he was great at wrecking careers and giving people criminal records so that they had even less chance of sorting their lives out, which increased their dependence on Absinthe. Lustus he got called in from time to time but he was small fry really. Unwanted pregnancies and STDs were his speciality. I was a freelancer for that mob you know. Not Absinthe's entire job list involved me."

"But you admit that you deceived people into taking action that would end their lives?"

"I don't know about admitting anything on the tape lady!"

"Dr Floss you smell like a bad BBQ where have you been?" Floss smirks at the DA's underhand tactics.

"OK, I admit it! I did tell them to do things that would potentially end their lives and I did encourage many others that didn't drink to end their lives too."

"And who else was involved in that racket? Asked Floss,

"Desparus, Culpus and Metus."

"So you worked freelance between two rackets, as did "Desparus, Culpus and Metus?"

"Yes"

"Interview terminated at 15:00 hours. Suicidus you are hereby charged with deliberately causing death by offering bad advice and you also stand charged of Genocide and racketeering. You will be held here up to the trial" states Petrova,

"take him back to his cell".

The guard remove Su and returns him to his cell. He can be heard demanding to know what level of the abyss he's going to get for his admission.

As Floss and Petrova leave the interview room they walk down the main corridor towards the refectory. As they walk along discussing their progress so far they bump into Gabriel.

"Archangel Gabriel. Is it possible that a request for a guardian Angel would go unheard?"

"Absolutely not, why what's going on?"

"This lady - Maria Escobar, she was found dead in an alleyway – cause of death – sever brain haemorrhage caused by a fall or push that smashed her skull open. She was severely inebriated also. Her mother requested a Guardian Angel for her when she was a baby but she wasn't protected from the fall."

"Well if the fall was brought on by the drinking, her angel would not have been able to do much on the grounds that she chose to drink. The question is whether or not she was pushed. The best person to speak to is Archangel Michael at the Angel training Camp headquarters, Mount Zion. He was in charge of all the Guardian angels back then. He will know which one you need to talk to.

"Thank you Archangel Gabriel" Floss replies gratefully. "I'll follow this lead up immediately".

Sparrow heads to the naturalization plant in Blackburn, Lancashire. A new lead has come in. A couple who lost their son in a car accident in 1980 have come forward to give evidence following media coverage of the high profile case.

Mr and Mrs Birtwistle sit waiting patiently for Sparrow in the offices of the naturalization project. Sparrow is shown into a quiet room and the elderly couple are ushered in.

"Good morning Thanks for offering to help with our investigation. What can you tell us about Absinthe and his mob?"

"Well our experience was with Absinthe himself. The boys were really too young to know the rest of them. They were only eighteen when they died."

"So what happened? Who died?"

"Our son Mark died on the 4th of October 1985. He was a passenger in a car driven by his friend Ben. There were five of them altogether in the vehicle at the time."

"What happened exactly?"

"They'd been out drinking since lunch time that day. The locals said that they'd been seen in the pub in Whalley drinking heavily from lunch time. They were all hard working lads. They were all at the same college studying engineering. Wednesdays they finished classes early and went to the pub."

"And how long did this go on for?"

"About eighteen months, they usually came home on the bus but this friend of theirs Ben had just passed his driving test and got his first car."

"What happened?"

"They were coming back along the main road at about 4pm. Witnesses said that they were going extremely fast and were all over the road. As the little car they were in approached the village Ben tried to overtake a vehicle in front of him. He was so drunk that he didn't see the school bus coming the other way. The force of the head on collision tilted the bus on its side as our boy and his four friends were sucked under the chassis and out the back of the bus in pieces."

Sparrow heaves at the thought of what she has just been told. Her eyes well up.

"Did any of them survive?

"Not one of them. The toxicologist's report showed that Ben was three times the legal driving limit at the time of impact".

"It must have been really hard for you both at the time."

"Betty...my wife broke down after mark's death....he was our only child.....I was so angry!....It wasn't just us, in hindsight ten parents lost children that day to Absinthe"

"The poor coach driver was off work for six months after the crash, he wasn't physically injured but mentally and emotionally it hit Him very hard. Some of the children on the bus were affected as well by what they saw."

"OK thank you Mr and Mrs Birtwistle. This is really helpful. Would you both be prepared to give evidence in the trial?"

"We most definitely would, yes!"

"Thank you, we will be in touch....Just one more thing Mr Birtwistle, do you remember the name of the pub that the boys were drinking in that day?"

"Yes miss the Hare and Hounds in Whalley."

"Thank you."

Swallow contacts headquarters to get the name of the landlord of the Hare and Hounds at the time of the accident. The information comes back to her and she makes her way to Clitheroe where the landlord is now living.

She knocks on the door of the old cottage and waits for a response,

"Yes love! What can I do for you?"

"My name's agent Sparrow FBI" She shows him her ID.

"Are you Albert The former landlord of the hare and Hounds in Whalley?"

"Yes I am, come in... what can I do for you? What does the FBI want with me! I cleaned up my act, that's why I'm still here!"

"You're not in trouble Albert", Sparrow smiles warmly, "I've just been talking to Mr and Mrs Birtwistle in Blackburn. Do you remember the accident?"

Albert's face drops as he recalls that tragic day.

"As if it were yesterday Miss Sparrow..."

Sparrow holds up the mug shot of Absinthe,

"Do you know this demon? She asks firmly,

"....Oh yes, I know him alright"

"Was he in your pub on the afternoon of the accident?"

Albert sits uncomfortably in his seats, he hesitates....

"Is he locked up now?"

"He is locked up Albert and he will remain so. Don't worry he can't get to you now."

"Obviously I didn't realise at the time, I didn't see it. In my old body we didn't have the powers to see did we miss sparrow but now we've all been upgraded I recall exactly what he was up to that afternoon."

"What happened Albert?"

"Mark and his friends came in about eleven thirty that morning. They finished college early on Wednesdays.......Absinthe was already sat at the bar when they came in. As soon as Ben approached the bar he was right next to him, patting him on the back, cracking silly jokes, encouraging him to drink as much as he could."

"How long did this go on for?"

"All afternoon, until about 3:30pm, Absinthe kept winding them all up; they got dafter and dafter as the drinks flowed."

"What happened just before they left?

"Mark and a couple of the other lads were talking about phoning a taxi....Absinthe kept telling Ben that he was the big man! That he could drive home safely with his mates and there'd be no problem. He could even drive faster now he was drunk because he had the racing driver skills to avoid all dangers! He really laid it on Ben and Ben being so young... I guess he believed it."

"Did Absinthe say anything else?"

"He kept going on at Ben about not leaving his car outside the pub because it might get stolen and reminding him that he needed it first thing in the morning."

"What happened after the boys left?"

"The rest of Absinthe's crew arrived. They had a right celebration that night......as news of the accident emerged they got rowdier and rowdier. Absinthe was boasting about how he set the driver up for that, hook line and sinker"

"Albert would you stand up in court and tell a jury what you've just told me?

"Yes I will miss"

"Thanks Albert I'll be in touch."

Angel training Camp Headquarters, Mount Zion.

Dr Floss waits patiently for Archangel Michael to arrive. He eventually turns up and shakes Floss's hand warmly.

"Good morning Dr. Floss."

"Morning Archangel Michael. Thanks for seeing me at such short notice. I'm trying to track down a Guardian Angel. He would have been appointed to this lady Maria Escobar, from Granada", Michael's ears prick up.

"Escobar...Escobar...yes of course.....she was Teetotaller's protégé. He nearly got court marshalled because of what happened with Maria. He was known as Curatio back then but Jesus himself intervened and changed his name to Teetotaller after she was found dead in that alley and Te was dragged away from the scene because he was just about to throttle Absinthe. Te claims that he witnessed Violensus murder Maria Escobar."

Floss suddenly gets very excited,

"Well that's it then we've got him. This should win the case for us!!"

"Don't get too excited Doctor. You obviously don't know much about Angel Law do you......Teetotaller may know perfectly well what happened in that alley but he is an angel. He can't give evidence in a human court of law.

Floss gets angry, "Damn it this is the best lead we've had so far", Michael looks shocked at Floss's blasphemy, "Sorry Archangel, excuse me",

Michael puts his hand on Floss's shoulder empathetically,

"Alex I understand how strongly you, all of us feel about this case. By all means go and talk to Te about Maria and what happened",

"Is there absolutely no way that Te could give evidence?" "If he was human he could",

"Well that's it then. There's not much point pursuing this line of investigation any further", replies Frost.

"Every Angel has the right to apply for humanisation. It is very rarely granted and is only ever granted under exceptional circumstances and I for one would not like to even hint that he would either want to or that he would be accepted, do you understand Doctor Floss? You must go and talk to him about it!"

Swallow returns home for a couple of days rest. It has been a long week travelling all over the globe and they've managed to collate some hefty evidence.

She lies on her hammock looking up at the clear blue sky and enjoying the warm sunshine beating down on her face. She begins to relax. Swallow is just dozing off when she wakes with a start. A sabre tooth tiger wanders into her plot and starts wondering around her hammock. She sits up slowly wondering how best to avoid being eaten alive but the huge wild animal comes up to her purring and sits at her feet. She very carefully puts her hand down and strokes its beautiful pearl coloured fur coat. The big cat rolls over affectionately with its legs up in the air. She climbs over her hammock and strokes the huge beast. It licks her face and purrs contentedly.

After a few minutes the cat stands up and walks off looking back at Swallow, beckoning her to follow. She follows the animal through the trees and out onto the new plain that has just been completed as part of the naturalisation process. Humans walking with wild animals that in the old world order were either extinct or would have eaten the humans for lunch. Children laughing and playing with Lions. Gorillas playing hide and seek with teenagers. People were busy preparing meals from the fruit in the trees. There was a huge lake were people were swimming. Some of the braver teenagers were hitching a ride on the back of an enormous crocodile. They thought it was hilarious. Even the crocodile looked as though it was enjoying itself.

Swallow enjoys two wonderful days of fellowship and is thrilled at how it seems the new world is going to be. She enjoys being with the animals, animals that she has only ever seen pictures of in books. The weekend though inevitably comes to an end and it's now time to go back to work.

Sparrow arrives in London at around 10am the morning after. She is on her way to see a young lady called Emma Harris. She arrives at the naturalisation project and Emma meets her at the entrance.

"Good morning Emma, nice to meet you" says Sparrow.

Emma greets her and they go off to find a quiet clearing in the project. Sparrow seems distracted at the overwhelming sight of the angels picking up tons of concrete and tarmac, bricks and mortar, cars, machinery everything and anything related to the old world order and bundling it into enormous containers after which it is transported to the fiery abyss in Jerusalem and dropped on top of its occupants.

"Here", says Emma. Attempting to get Sparrow's attention again.

"Sorry!" Sparrow snaps out her trance and jumps to the task at hand,

"OK, so you say that you had dealings with Absinthe and his mob Emma, because of your father Bill?"

"Yes my dad. Absinthe got into his life when I was about twelve. Up until then he was a great guy, friendly and fun. He'd always had bouts of depression, so my mum said and apparently his childhood was not great but most of the time he was fine.

"What do you remember Emma?"

"My dad was about thirty four when the drinking started. He began going to the pub a couple of nights a week for a drink or two and he would come back merry. This was no problem to start with. He was quite funny after a couple. Then it started getting later and later for a few months until my mum and him had a big argument about him never being in until gone eleven o'clock at night. After that he was straight home after work but he started drinking a lot at home. He would sit there with Absinthe and drink a couple of cans before dinner and then carry on drinking into the early hours. Usually until he fell asleep at his table. Absinthe used to egg him on to wind my mum up or me and my sisters. He'd start bullying us verbally when he had had a lot to drink"

"Did your mum ever challenge him about Absinthe and the drinking?"

"Once she did and he flipped. Violensus was there that night. He egged my dad on to totally trash the kitchen and he hit my mum and threatened my older sister. Absinthe sat their roaring with laughter thinking it was hilarious."

"What happened after that?"

"My mum left for a couple of days and took us with her to our Nan's". They sorted out their differences though and for a while there was no sign of Absinthe but Desparus and Metus were round more and more often. They just sat their taunting my dad and making him feel more and more miserable. They kept telling him that he couldn't manage without Absinthe."

"And then? Asked Swallow expectantly,

"He eventually gave in and let Absinthe back in. This time though more of them turned up as well. A big fat ugly one called Sloth started coming round early morning, telling my dad to stop in bed and skip looking for work. Desparus and Metus kept turning up and another one, this one here", Emma points to the picture of Culpus,

"Culpus" Swallow clarified.

"Yes that's him. Over time they wore my dad down to the ground. They would really lay the pressure onto him during the day, especially after he lost his licence for drunk driving and then his job. Absinthe started to arrive earlier and earlier until eventually my dad was drinking at breakfast."

"How long did this go on for?"

"Until I was about sixteen. In the end my dad was only a shadow of the man he used to be. One night they were all there living it large. My dad was shouting at my mum and being so abusive. My mum told him to get out. He stood up to hit my mum again but I put myself between him and mum and stood up to him. He picked up a carving knife off the kitchen top and threatened me with it. My little sister called the police from her mobile phone in her bedroom. The police burst in and arrested him. He was sent to jail."

"What affect did this have on your mother, you and your sisters?"

"My mother was in so much debt now because of my dad's drinking. The house was repossessed because my dad hadn't worked for twelve months. Sloth just convinced him to stay home and not look for work. He made all sorts of excuses about being ill and depressed."

"What happened next?"

"He came out of jail and went into a bail hostel because my mum didn't want him back. He was drinking very heavily in the hostel. He wouldn't talk to me or my sister. He blamed us for landing him in jail. Culpus had blinded him to the truth."

"What truth?"

"That his own actions had landed in the mess he was in!"

replied Emma angrily,

"So to what extent do you think that this mess was your dad's fault Emma? This is important because this is what the case against Absinthe and his cronies is all about "Free Will!"

Emma thought about the question.

"I guess....although my dad chose to drink to start with....there came a stage where he became dependent on Absinthe, he was such a charmer that bastard!" Emma breaks down in tears; Swallow puts her arms around her, "its ok!"

"Culpus, Desparus, Metus and Sloth ran rings around my dad. They made his life a living hell and he didn't know what was going on, none of us knew at the time!"

"How did it all end for your dad?"

"He disappeared from the bail hostel for about two weeks. Nobody knew where he was. He'd broken the conditions of his bail. When they found him he was taken to hospital in a really bad state. His liver was packing in. He was jaundiced. He was then transferred to a prison hospital near Liverpool. He died in hospital after about six weeks."

"How did you all feel when you found out?"

"Heart broken I guess...yet relieved at the same time....he wasn't be bullied by those ass-holes anymore."

"Emma would you be prepared to give evidence in court? To stand up and say what you've said to me in front of a jury?"

"Yes I would".

"Thanks Emma, we'll be in touch."

Back in Washington at the Courts of Justice the morning has come were Absinthe's application for bail is to be heard. Absinthe and his mob are escorted by angel guardians to the court house.

Petrova the District Attorney and the Attorney General Miles Hamilton wait nervously in the courtroom for Absinthe, his cronies and their brief to arrive.

The atmosphere in the court room is electric as angel and human journalists crowd outside the courtroom waiting for Absinthe to arrive.

The guardian angels suddenly land in front of the entrance and Absinthe and his mob are swarmed by reporters. Absinthe in true form plays up to the interest that everyone is showing in him and start bowing like a cabaret star before his expectant audience.

"Rumour has it that you you've been indicted on charges of genocide Absinthe, how are you going to plead in the case?"

"Absolutely not guilty. Most of you guys new me in the old world order. I'm just an entertainer! Did I ever tell you guys to drink too much? never!"

The court room ushers push Absinthe through the crowds to the entrance of the court?"

"Do you think you'll get bail?" shouts another reporter.

"Who knows, we'll see what my brief can do uuhh!"

John meets Absinthe and his cronies in the accused section of the chambers.

"Hey John you going to get us out of here my friend?"

John looks nervously at Absinthe and his crew and sits down in front them.

"Absinthe it's not looking good. Jesus himself is the judge in this case and the evidence that's started coming back in already is pretty damning."

Absinthe gets irate,

"Hey you're my attorney and it's your job to get us out of here, come on John!"

"I'll do what I Absinthe but I can suggest you guys don't hold your breath. The court's about to go into session come on."

As Absinthe and his cronies enter the courtroom they are blinded by a pure brilliant light. The jury of seraphim have assembled in the courtroom to witness the start of this case and the highest ranking of all the Seraphim will communicate directly with Jesus himself. No humans are allowed within a 50ft of the Seraphim as even their new eyes would not be able to withstand this celestial light. Each Seraphim has six wings: two with which they cover their faces, two with which they cover their feet, and two for flying.

Abs suddenly looks overwhelmed. He looks at his cronies sat at the bench next to him,

"I've not seen these guys since we got booted out of heaven with Satan!"

"Yes, they must be taking this really seriously if Jesus himself is going to judge this case boss." says Desparus,

"Just keep quiet and we'll be ok. Plead ignorance."

The court room go deadly quiet and the chief Seraphim stands.

"Absinthe, Sloth, Lustus, Violensus, Desparus, Culpus, Metus and Suicidus. You stand here accused of genocide and multiple war crimes against humanity, resisting arrest and psychological warfare. The purpose of this case is to discern which level of the abyss you should be assigned to for the next thousand years. How you do you all plead?"

"Not guilty" says Suicidus,

"Not guilty" says Desparus,

"Not guilty" says Violensus,

"Not guilty" says Lustus,

"Not guilty" says Sloth,

"Not guilty!" says Absinthe,

John starts his plea for bail.

"Your honour my clients would like you to ask The Anointed One for bail."

"Your honour bail has never in the history of the earth been granted for mass murder, let alone genocide and multiple war crimes against humanity." adds Petrova.

"On what grounds?" asks the chief Seraphim, "They stand accused of genocide, a most serious and deplorable crime against humanity."

The sweat pours of John's brow as he thinks on his feet.

"Your honour, bearing in mind that alcohol is now a banned substance in the new world order. I would argue that my clients are no danger to the public any more, if ever they were....... and should therefore be granted bail until the court case."

The Seraphim does not respond immediately. After a few minutes,

"Very well, your clients have two choices. The third level of the abyss for the duration of the trial or their present residence on Alcatraz Island."

The court erupts with laughter from the humans in the court as they observe the look of disappointment on their faces. John tries so hard not to grin and let his clients know how happy he is that they are not going to walk free. He confers with his clients....

"My clients wish to return to Alcatraz your honour."

"Very well. Would the defence and prosecution please approach the bench?"

John and Petrova approach the bench. They have to wear special glasses to protect their eyes.

"How long is the investigation going to take?" asks the Seraphim?

Petrova responds, "about another month your honour"

"OK"

"The trial will start in one month from now. Court is adjourned. Take them down."

Absinthe and his crew are taken out of the courtroom via a back door to avoid the press and taken back to Alcatraz Island. The humans in the court room cheer as the demons are taken back into custody.

Petrova and Gabriel look at each other and breathe a sigh of relief that bail was not granted.

As Absinthe is escorted past Gabriel he can't resist,

"You can't avoid the heat for ever Abs; make the most of your little island while it lasts!" Violensus tries to break free from the guards and attack Gabriel who flies backwards to avoid him. The guards overpower Violensus and drag him out of the court room. PETRONAS's ambivalent glance at Gabriel is a mixture of amusement and disapproval and Gabriel looks up into the sky sheepishly.

John leaves the courtroom feeling very alienated. He doesn't even want to represent these thugs but he holds on to his faith that good will come from this in the end.

Back at Alcatraz Absinthe has demanded to see John. He arrives looking miserable at the summons.

"John what happened?" demands Absinthe,"I thought you was going to get us out of here?"

"The Seraphim made it quite clear. You should have been in the abyss but you resisted arrest when Jesus returned. This place is your only respite." replies John worriedly.

"Let's not forget our little secret John" whispers Absinthe.

"John looks at Absinthe with a look of horror on his face",

"I'm doing my best for you all Absinthe!" replies join pleadingly,

"Make sure you do!"

Prypiat. Ukraine

Once home to over 50,000 people this city once housed the workers of the Chernobyl nuclear plant until its meltdown in 1986. The city was what had come to be known as the Zone of Alienation, the 30 km radius surrounding Chernobyl, it is quite literally dead. Teetotaller and a team of Ukrainian bounty hunters are looking for another rogue demon that has been spotted hiding out in the city.

Swallow is brought in by an angel Navigator.

Teetotaller has been briefed about his visitor and greets Swallow on her arrival.

"Good flight Miss Swallow?" asks Te,"How was your flight?"

"Easier than it used to be", Swallow thanks the navigator and asks him to wait. She looks at Te and suddenly feels very uncomfortable, shy even,

"I believe you already know why I'm here Te? Can you help us?" She ask very formally

"If I can I will. What do you want to know?" Te smiles at her, she avoids his glance.

"The night Maria Escobar died where you were?"

"In France, I got back to Granada just in time to see what happened. Absinthe and his cronies had led Maria down this alley way in the student quarter. They were pushing her about, bullying her. She was weeping and upset. I saw Violensus walk up behind her and push her really hard onto the floor. She smashed her head on a curb stone."

"And this is when you lost your temper and flew at Absinthe?"

"Yes, I'd looked after Maria since she was born and saved her life on numerous occasions when the incident was not caused by her own free will."

"What about the time when she was drunk driving? That was by her own free will?" asks Swallow.

"Yes but there were two other souls involved in that incident as well Miss Swallow, remember? Her baby and an innocent lorry driver. Furthermore my intervention didn't protect her from the consequences of her own actions. She was arrested, lost her licence, wrecked her car. She suffered a lot and so did her loved ones.

"How strongly do you feel about Maria and what happened to her?" asks Swallow very formally,

"Very strongly. I captured Abs in Blackpool, as you probably already know. Any way I hope my statement helps. Pity I can't give evidence, being an angel and all, it's impossible."

"There is a way.....but it would change the course of your life forever....you could apply for humanisation"

Teetotaller looks confused.

"I don't understand how do I go about humanising?"

"You have to apply to the Seraphim and if successful you'd have to undergo a serious operation to have your wings removed and to be gendered....of course it's not reversible. If you do it you would be a human for eternity from then on.....think about it Te and let me know, don't decide here and now."

"OK, I will. Do you have to get off straight away or can you hang around for a while?" Te asks warmly. Swallow looks embarrassed. "I...guess I could stay for the day".

"Great, come on! We are just about to catch this demon Periculum, alias "The Gambler". He's not a dangerous character, just a stubborn pain in the back side. He's hiding in them buildings over there."

"OK, I'll sit here and watch" says swallow nervously trying to deny the feelings that are welling up inside her for this ANGEL! "I don't believe in love at first sight." she tries to convince herself. I can't fall for an Angel!

"Come on Periculum! Time to go!" shouts Te, winking at Swallow with a smile on his face. She looks down, avoiding his eyes.

"I bet you 3-1 you can't catch me!" shouts Periculum from the ruins.

"You're already surrounded on all sides and from above. Your odds are not that much in your favour today, so come on! It's freezing in this God forsaken city!"

"Periculum suddenly makes a break. He flies up out of the ruins and tries to escape. Two guardians throw a net over him, covering his wings and he hits the ground, money and betting cards flying everywhere.

"Game over Periculum" Te shouts sarcastically as he is tied up and taken away to the Abyss.

"Where are you headed next?" asks Te, looking longingly at Swallow.

"Burnley, in Lancashire."

"Can I drop you off?"

"I couldn't possibly let you..."

"It would be my pleasure, Miss Swallow."

"OK" says Swallow nervously.

The Final Witness

Te drops Swallow off in Burnley. He lands by the canal and smiles at her.

"Could I meet you again", he asks?

Swallows smiles, "But you are an Angel!" Te sighs, "true, true, look we can just meet up to go for a walk or something?"

"OK", says Swallow nervously. "I'll contact you when I have finished taking statements. This may be the last one."

"OK, I'll hold you to that." Te takes swallows hand affectionately and remembers his status and quickly lets go. He flies up and waves at Swallow and flies off."

An ex drug and alcohol rehabilitation worker has come forward to give evidence.

Swallow meets the ex drug worker Karl Fenn near the old Leeds to Liverpool canal on what used to be Colne road. The house they are going into is a large gloomy looking end terrace that is elevated above the canal. It used to be a boarding house.

Swallow greets Karl

"Good morning Karl. So you're going to tell me about Absinthe and his mob?"

"Yes, I worked here as a drug and alcohol rehabilitation worker for twenty years before the return of Jesus." Karl shows Swallow around the gloomy old house. There's a repugnant stench that hits you as soon as you walk through the door, it's a melange of urine, alcohol and rotting flesh.

"Sorry about the smell Miss Swallow. Incontinence is one of the later stage symptoms of alcohol abuse. The poor men and women that were in here were all addicted to alcohol or drugs of one type or another."

"It smells like death....if death can be defined by a smell!"

"Well you're probably not far from the truth there Miss Swallow. Many of the residents who were in here left in body bags. They'd drown in their own vomit or fall and hit their heads. Quite often they wouldn't be found for a day or two and by that stage the smell had got into the carpets or the beds."

Swallow runs outside and vomits over the railings into the canal. The stench is so bad that it has turned her stomach upside down.

Karl stands behind her waiting patiently. He hands her an ointment to rub under her nose. "This will take your mind off the smell."

They re-enter the property. As they go from room to room Swallow takes memory photos of the graffiti on the walls. 'Life is shit', 'I wish I were dead', she memory videos the graffiti, the empty bottles of vodka and the rusting cans of ale that lie scattered around the floor.

"So tell me about Absinthe and his mob?"

"They were always here, always. We obviously didn't see them back then before we got our upgraded bodies but now looking back all the blanks have been filled in. They were permanent residents."

"How did they operate?" sparrow continues collating evidence as she listens.

"Desparus, Culpus and Metus used to badger all the residents 24/7. They were real bullies. Sloth used to make it easy for them to stay home and do nothing. He showed them every trick in the book to get easy money. Absinthe didn't do much entertaining when he was here. He just told them over and over again that they needed him and they'd listen and obey...otherwise Desparus would come on really hard and Metus would scare the life out of them."

"What about this one here – Suicidus?" She shows him the mug shot.

"He'd visit about two or three time a year. See that hole up there in the ceiling Miss Swallow. One guy ripped the plaster off the ceiling there and looped the belt of his dressing gown round that exposed beam. Hung himself. Nobody found him for three day and that was only because the smell got so bad."

"Was this place not staffed 24/7?" asked swallow whilst taking a mental photo of the ceiling,

"Funding was very scarce in the end times and guys like me we worked on a rota system visiting about thirty different homes like this, in the course of a week. We knew all the funerals directors in Lancashire because we liaised with at least two different ones every week."

"Do you know this one? Swallow shows Karl a mug shot of Lustus.

"Oh yes, we got a lot of working girls in here. Their main demon was Cocainas; he was another one that spent most of his time here. He was in cahoots with Absinthe. Lustus would bring men in off the streets for the girls so that they could score and feed their habits. Is he on trial as well?"

"No he's already in the abyss and he's way down on the lower levels already and hasn't even tried to claim 'Free will'".

"Well how could he!" replies the drug worker. "Absinthe was an evil bastard but Cocainas, he was ruthless. Where Absinthe would bide his time and real them in slowly, Cocainas raped them almost immediately and that was it! Once they were hooked they were hooked big time and it was very difficult to get off it."

"What's this white stick here?" "There was one guy who lost his sight because of the drinking. He used to walk around bumping into walls. When you're blind drunk and visually blind you don't have, much of a leg to stand on really. Eventually Violensus tripped him up when he was trying to come down stairs. My co-worker found him dead here," he points to the bottom of the stairs where there are some cracks in the floor tiles.

"Did his fall cause these tiles to crack?"

"We think so..."

"He must have been pushed with a hell of a force."

Karl and swallow make their way back outside the building.

"Karl would you be prepared to give evidence alongside the memory evidence that I've collected here today."

"I certainly would."

"That's great I'll be in touch soon."

Swallow is carried away by an angel navigator back to headquarters.

The Life & Times of Cocainas and Heroinas

Unlike Absinthe who was very cultured and subtle in his approach to the kill, these two demons were ruthless and vulgar in their approach. Absinthe would bide his time and get his victims hooked over a longish period of time. Between twelve months to three, five maybe ten years. Cocainas and Heroinas went straight in for the hook. One or two goes and they were addicted, totally addicted. If they didn't continue to buy the drugs Culpus, Metus and Desparus would be right there bullying their victims into submission. The physical effects of withdrawal from these drugs included horrible side affects like headaches and depression.

Furthermore Cocainas and Heroinas were much more prone to initiating sudden assassinations rather than prolonging the agony. They would mix their poisons with all sorts of things like rat poison or other nasty chemicals just to thicken it out and make it go further. Many of their victims would shoot up and die on the spot from a bad fix.

The Social Services didn't bother snatching children from drug dealers. The new perfectly well who they were but it was all political. Revenue from drugs was big business that transcended all classes of society.

The dealers were very crafty in their tactics at keeping people hooked. If an addict was making an effort to give it up the dealer would just give her a fix for free, in her hand. That would be too much temptation and they would be right back to square one.

Sometimes whole families would become addicted to these drugs. Addicts would sometimes send their children out to steal food or beg for money. They would then bring the money back and it would be used to pay Cocainas and Heroinas.

The pair were not above targeting children directly either. They gave the dealers the idea of putting the drugs in sweets and other things that kids liked.

Chapter 8

Preparing the Prosecution

Dr Floss and the District attorney sit looking over the evidence that Agent Swallow has collected over the last ten days.

"This is great stuff. The behavioural patterns of this mob are all the same or very similar. Real them in, break them down and spit them out", explains Floss.

"We really need Teetotaller to stand up in court and give evidence. Have you heard anything from him about humanising?" asks Petrova.

"No not as yet. He could actually clinch the whole case because angels can't lie. Let's just pray he does decide to go ahead and humanise!" adds Floss.

"We can now question Absinthe and his crew, present them with the evidence we'll use against them and see if they want to change their pleas. In your opinion doctor, which one of these demons is mostly likely to cave in under pressure?"

Floss thinks about the question for a couple of minutes.

"I'd say Sloth...he hates being under any stress or pressure. His philosophy is anything for an easy life."

"OK let's question them one at a time and try and break sloth for a confession!"

The Interviews

A special interview room has been set up to question the demons about their involvement in all these cases.

The first one in is Desparus (1) with John his attorney. Floss and Petrova sit at one end of the table. Desparus is told to sit at the other.

"My name is Helga Petrova; I'm the DA leading the case for the prosecution. This is Dr. Floss who is overseeing the investigation."

"I got nothing to say."

"Do you remember Helen Brown, Desparus? She knows you!...in her statement she claims that you used to go round there every morning after Absinthe had been there and bully her into a depression?"

"I never met the woman"

"Oh we'll see about that", replies Floss,

You were seen by Helen every time that Absinthe had been round, you were there! I'm going to get the truth out of your friends Desparus so you may as well come clean now!"

"I never met her!"

Did you used to taunt Helen Brown until she gave into absinthe?

"I never met her!"

"OK, did you meet these people here Desparus in this boarding house in Burnley Lancashire?" Petrova shows Desparus the pictures of the one hundred and fifty victims that died there.

"No, never"

"But you were seen! Remember Karl the support worker. He's one of the faithful ones and risen." Desparus' mouth drops,

"You were seen Desparus. Do you recognise this writing?" Floss turns on a holographic image of the graffiti that Swallow copied off the walls of the house. 'Life is shit', "that's your writing isn't it Desparus, in fact this has got your name written all over it! Only you could make somebody feel like that!" adds Floss.

"No comment!" says Desparus looking worried.

"Did you have a good time in sunny Spain Desparus? Do you remember Maria Escobar", her picture appears in the hologram, "Her husband remembers you!...says you were round there every morning until Absinthe arrived! He can see you now he has his upgraded body Desparus!"

"No comment."

"You were seen by Teetotaller when Maria was murdered, that makes you an accessory to murder if nothing else! If Teetotaller decides to humanise, he'll be giving evidence against you to that affect!"

"Screw you!" reply Desparus aggressively,

"You had a little run in that night with Teetotaller didn't you?"

"I don't remember any Teetotaller!"

"Curatio!"

"That schmuck...huh"

"So you admit to having a run in with Curatio?"

John intervenes,"that's a very leading question!"

"So did you have a run in with Curatio?"

Desparus doesn't answer. The interview is suspended for the time being to see what the other demons have to say.

Culpus

The second one in is Culpus (1), with John. Floss and Petrova sit at one end of the table. Culpus is told to sit at the other.

"Do you remember Maria Escobar, Culpus?" asks Floss

"No", replies Culpus

"Her husband says that you used to spend a lot of time round at her place, bullying her until she gave into Absinthe? Says you really hounded her about losing her licence?"

"You can't prove a thing!"

"You were seen! What's more Curatio heard you blame Maria for everything moments before Violensus push her over?"

"What does he know? He got there after she was pushed"

"SO YOU WERE THERE!?"

Culpus regrets opening his mouth."No comment" he replies.

"Let's see. Helen Brown...did you tell her that she was a bad person and that all the shit in her life was her own fault?"

"I don't remember"

"She remembers, as if it was yesterday! The night she died you laid into her about losing her job didn't you? You didn't tell her that it was partly Sloth's fault for deceiving her!"

"No comment!"

"Another young lady that knows you – Emma Harris...remember her Culpus? You played a large part in destroying her father's life and her family's by laying the guilt trips on him didn't you?!

"Prove it!"

"We will", replies Floss confidently, "remember the boarding house on Colne Rd, Burnley!? The support worker remembers you Culpus. YOU WERE

SEEN, DAMN IT, JUST COME CLEAN!" Petrova is getting very frustrated. John insists that his client is given a break as the interview has gone on for some time. Culpus is sent back to his cell for the time being.

Metus

The third one in is Metus (1), with John, his attorney. Floss sits at one end of the table and Petrova wonders relentlessly around the room. Metus is told to sit at the other end. Petrova starts the interview.

"Metus, well, well, well, demon of fear! You've got a colourful record haven't you sunshine!!

"Bog off!" replies Metus.

"Flattery will get you nowhere. Do you remember Helen Brown Metus?"

"Maybe"

"You deceived her into thinking that she'd lose her job for drinking the night before, is that correct?" asks floss.

"No"

She claims you did. What about Bill Harris? Do you remember him? You spent a lot of time there didn't you making his life a misery. You encouraged him to scare his wife and children!

"No that was Violensus, not me!"

"So Violensus scared Bill's wife and children?"

"Yes"

"Interview suspended at 11:15pm. We'll be back to you shortly."

"Take him back down", shouts Petrova, "bring up Violensus please.

Violensus (1) is brought in completely wrapped up in duck tape and tied to an old parcel trolley.

"Violensus," says Petrova very calmly.

"You've been accused of murdering Maria Escobar, amongst millions of others worldwide in all the wars you've helped to create. You were seen on the night Maria died to push her over causing her to have a brain haemorrhage that killed her. How do you plead?

"Not guilty",

"Violensus you were seen" replies Floss calmly.

"What about this blind man at the boarding house in Burnley? The support worker says that you were always there. The position he was led in is inconsistent with a mere fall. He was pushed violently. The damage to those tiles at the bottom of the stairs – here", the hologram displays the image, "suggests your handy work Violensus!"

"Bullshit!"

"Language Violensus, we do have grottier cells here than the one you are in....Remember Bill Harris Violensus. His daughter says that you put Bill up to terrifying his wife and children?

"No...never"

"Violensus...Metus says that you put Bill up to terrifying his wife and children" Violensus gets angry and struggles against the duck tape.

"The dirty rotten grass I'll kill him!"

"Well you could try but I don't think it would get you very far. You're all going to the abyss. What remains to be decided is which level you are all going to." adds Floss.

"We also have a witness that saw you murder Maria Escobar down that back alley in Granada Violensus! would you like to change your plea?"

"Not in this life time" laughs Violensus

"Pleading guilty and admitting everything now would guarantee you a higher level in the abyss. Think about that for now!

Violensus is wheeled back to a grottier cell for swearing and to hopefully encourage him to consider coming clean.

The fifth one in is Sloth (1) with John, his attorney. Floss sits at one end of the table and Petrova stands behind him. Sloth is told to sit at the other end. Floss starts the interview.

"Do you remember Helen Brown Sloth?"

"No"

"She remembers you. She claims that you deceived her. You convinced her that it would be better to stay home from work because she'd been with Absinthe the night before"

"She made her own choices!"

"That's not quite true though is it Sloth? Desparus, Culpus and Metus were there making her life a misery...weren't they?"

Sloth says nothing. He sits with his arms folded. Floss looks at Petrova.

"What about Maria Escobar Sloth. Remember her? She remembers you! You told her not to worry about her house and stuff didn't you?" Sloth remains silent...

"Bill Harris? You told him to stay home and not bother looking for work...what's more you were known to be a permanent resident at the boarding house on Colne road in Burnley...the support worker....Karl/...you remember?....he's testifying against you Sloth!

"No comment", replies Sloth smugly.

Petrova looks ready to make her move and go for check mate.

"Sloth there's a level in the abyss that would suite you down to the ground. You'd spend the next thousand years carrying debris from the bottom of the abyss to the top and then more debris from the top to the bottom...24/7 Sloth for a thousand years.....You might lose some weight in the process...seems a good place for a lazy, bone idle demon like you to.."OK, OK I'll talk, I'll talk! If you can guarantee that I won't have to do any work in the abyss....I'll talk"

"No sorry Sloth its hard labour for you!" replies Petrova, Sloth looks dumbfounded now...

"I'll talk, come on!"

"Give evidence in court then...against all of them?" asks Petrova cautiously.

"OK, but I want protection whilst I'm in here"

Petrova addresses the guard at the door,

"Take Sloth to one of the staff apartments on the upper level. Keep him under armed guard. He's now a witness."

Petrova looks triumphantly at Floss as Sloth is taken away. They make their way to Absinthe's cell to question him about the evidence that has snow emerged.

They enter absinthe's cell.

"Well well, it's Bat man and Robin", mocks Absinthe

"I'd wipe that smile off your face if I were you Absinthe", replies Petrova.

"Oh yea and why is that?"

"Oh, let' see.....Remember Mark Birtwistle Abs, Whalley, Lancashire?"

"No can't say I do"

"The Hare and Hounds public house?"

"Yea, vaguely."

"Mark and four of his friends were drinking in that pub the day they died. Where were you at the time?"

Abs hesitates, thinking carefully about his response.

"I can't remember"

"Oh that's a shame because the landlord of The Hare and Hounds remembers you being there. You were best friends with Ben, the driver, that day weren't you?"

"That's my job, I'm an entertainer. If he got drunk that his problem. I didn't tell him to."

"Maybe not but you did convince him to drive. You made him think that he was Nigel Mansell, that he was some super human driver!"

"Well he made his own choices."

"Based on lies that you deceived him with! That his car might get stolen and that he needed the car in the morning. Why didn't you remind him that his dad had a car and would have dropped him off at his car in the morning?!" asks Petrova.

"I didn't know that"

"Don't lie to me Abs! You were heard talking to your cronies later, after the boys had been killed, saying, I quote, "I set them up hook, line and sinker."

"Who heard me say that?!" he asks defiantly. "Albert, the landlord of the pub." replies Floss.

Absinthe sits and says nothing. "What about Maria Escobar Absinthe. Her husband says, I quote, from his statement,

'that son of bitch Absinthe would simply hold out his arms and comfort Maria, even though towards the end he would make her drink so much before he would do anything for her'.... How do you explain this Abs? A lot of people are very pissed off with you?"

"She threw the liquor down her throat, not me."

"No Absinthe, you got her hooked and then withdrew your affection and let your cronies Desparus, Metus and Culpus torture her until she gave in and had another drink. Tell the truth Abs! Plead guilty and you might get a lighter sentence."

"No chance. It's all circumstantial"

"One of your cronies has ratted on you Abs. He's going to testify against you. How do you feel about that?

"A load of crap! Scare tactics!"

"Remember the boarding house in Burnley, Colne road? The support worker

Karl. He's going to testify as well."

Absinthe remains silent.

"Do you want to change your plea at this stage Abs?"

"I want my lawyer!"

Petrova terminates the interview. John is summoned back to Alcatraz. In the meantime Suicidus is brought back again for questioning?

"How much evidence are you prepared to give us Su? Demands Petrova.

"What level of the abyss will I get?

"Higher than if you refuse to give evidence.

"Can I think about it?" asks Su.

"Take your time, you're not going anywhere" replies Petrova.

Swallow has some well earned time off now and contacts Te about that walk. He flies over to meet her and takes her to Austria where the mountains and countryside remain unspoiled.

They walk around the mountains and hills and visit the beautiful, unspoiled little villages that remain, untouched by the old world order.

They stop to have something to eat. They pick fruit off the trees and drink water from the natural springs that flow down the mountainside.

At night time Te takes Swallow over the Assad volcanic field in north east Africa which is erupting at the moment.

Afterwards they fly over the Grand Canyon and on to South America, then Motuo in China and then Australia. After a full day of flying around, chatting and getting to know each other, the pair are getting on really well. They fly under the falls at Niagara and wonder about in the caves underneath.

"If only you were human, we could have a better relationship," Swallow looks sad for a moment. Te takes her hand.

"I could humanise. It's a complicated process but not impossible."

"I couldn't possibly ask you to do that for me!"

"Well I'll be a lonely Angel stuck here on my own for the next thousand years."

"You're very presumptuous thinking that I'll want to be with you for the next thousand years", Swallows says, in an embarrassed tone of voice.

"Would you really do that for me?"

"I'll look into it, definitely." Swallow and Te hug for a few minutes but a storm cloud starts to develop over them so they stop and Te takes her back to headquarters

The 'Expert' Witness for the Defence.

John needs to come up with something fast for the defence. He is struggling because there aren't many people who are prepared to defend Abs and his cronies, not out of the saved at least. The best he can do is to find someone who is adamant that these drinkers only had themselves to blame. John's team of defence lawyers scour the records of people who worked with alcoholics and he comes up with a social worker who was apparently obsessed with taking their children off them. The problem is she is in the Abyss. Andrea Fay was a ruthless, humourless, career social worker who worked her way to the top by searching out children for middle class couples.

The prettier the children, the more determined she would become to seize them, even if it meant lying through her teeth. Every child she snatched was another notch on her belt, another merit from her superiors. For some reason which is now so obvious. Satan was in charge back then. They never went after the children who were living with drug dealers. Cocainas wouldn't allow it but Absinthe and Desparus were quite happy for Andrea and her team of carers to assist them in their destruction of people's lives.

She lived in Pendle Forest in Lancashire, England and historically was related to the famous Pendle Witch Chattox.

Of an evening she would be seen cavorting round a cauldron on Pendle Hill with her colleagues and would hold case conferences up there with Absinthe and his cronies to see who they could victimise next and how.

John arrives at the Abyss and asks for Andrea Fay to be brought out for questioning. The guardian angels working on the gates look at each other confused. They talk amongst themselves.

"You're sure you want this one?! She's a nasty piece of work."

"Yes. She worked with the drinkers."

"OK, it's your call!"

Fay is brought to Alcatraz by a navigator and ushered into an interview room with John. She sits, straight faced and emotionless at the table, brushing the ash of her smoking face and arms.

"What do you want? Who are you?" John jumps back in his seat at her abruptness.

"I want to question you about the work you did with the alcoholics? I need you as an expert witness in a case between The People v Absinthe and his colleagues."

"Why should I help you?!"

"You may get a better place in the Abyss for your troubles."

"OK, well as long as there is something in it for me. I'm used to doing deals with lawyers." She smiles and winks. John looks uncomfortable but starts the questioning. There was a time when negotiating with social workers for children was a lucrative business but after becoming a Christian John tried to stop all that kind of dodgy dealing.

"The prosecution's case is based on allegations that Absinthe and his colleagues worked as a team to break down and destroy the lives of their victims. What is your perception of them Miss Fay."

"Who? Absinthe or the drinkers?

"The drinkers. What do you want me to say? I'm sure Absinthe and his friends did them over left right and centre. They kept us in children all the time. We never had any problems with them." John looks disappointed and angry at what he's hearing.

"I can't believe that...are you saying that you would lie in court to help defend them if it will better your position in the Abyss!?

"Why not! I lied all my life. If I'm stuck in the Abyss for a thousand years I may as well do what I can for myself."

John remains silent. "Well Smith? Shall I fabricate a pack of lies for you?"

"You can remain here for the time being on Alcatraz. I may need to call you as a witness." John leaves the interview room disgusted at what he has just heard.

Chapter 9

The Betrayal

11Have nothing to do with the fruitless deeds of darkness, but rather expose them**12** it is shameful even to mention what the disobedient do in secret. **13** But everything exposed by the light becomes visible—and everything that is illuminated becomes a light.

Ephesians 5:11

John nervously returns to Absinthe's cell. His heart is pounding. His nerves are shot at. He enters the cell and sits in the usual place.

"I'm just wondering why I feel like you're not doing your job John" Absinthe says very calmly. Sweat pouring off his brow, John replies....."It no good Abs...In all honesty...they've got you all...you may as well plead guilty and hope for a lighter sentence than you'll get if you continue to drag this out."

"Who has ratted on us John?"

"I can't tell you that. I'm sworn to secrecy. He's in witness protection now." replies John nervously. He bites his nails and fidgets in his seat.

"I don't need to remind you, do I? about our little secret John!" whispers absinthe, "you never did overcome your cravings for whisky did you? Even after you joined Jesus' side you kept drinking secretly right up to the end of the old world order!", "Shut it Absinthe! Do you realise what would happen to all of us if this got out!?"

"Who has betrayed me John?" asks Absinthe again. "I can't tell you", "Who has betrayed me John? I know where you can find some bottles of scotch that haven't been confiscated yet. They're hidden about 200 yards from here John. It's been a long time since you had a drink hasn't it!? Think about the fun we could have again! Just like the good old days."

"Sloth", whispers John under his breath.

"I knew I couldn't trust that fat moron!", Absinthe discloses the location of the hidden whisky and John leaves the cell, composing himself so as not to draw attention to his agitation. Absinthe gives him a note and tells him to pass it on to Suicidus on his way down the corridor. John slips the note to Suicidus.

He can't get the liquor off his mind now, yet he feels ambivalent as he considers his relationship with God, his betrayal of Sloth and the code of legal conduct that he used to swear by, that he has now just broken for a shallow reward.

John returns to his apartment. He sits at the table unsure what to do. He remembers 'the good old days' that Abs was referring to. "Just one drink and

I'll be able to focus on this case. Even if we don't win it will see me through until it's all over" John thinks to himself, "but the betrayal – oh shit, what have I done to my God, to my career. I need a drink!" John starts to tremble as the old feelings start to come back.

0300 hrs. Suicidus' Prison Cell

It's all quiet in the prison wing where Absinthe's crew are being held.

Suicidus sits up quietly. He squeezes through the bars of his cell and flies up into the ventilation shaft above. He quietly makes his way through the maze of pipes up to the staff apartments on the upper level. He locates Sloth's cell and creeps into his apartment. He sees Sloth led there in his new warm comfortable bed. He hovers over Sloth and puts one foot over Sloth's mouth, bringing the other down with a great force onto Sloth's stomach.

Sloth's eyes open with a look of shock and pain. He sees Suicidus stood over him.

"Rat on us will you, you son of a bitch!!" whispers Suicidus. Sloth struggles but Su's foot is firmly over him mouth.

"Withdraw your statement and refuse to give evidence or I'll be back tomorrow morning to finish you off you fat pig! Capice?" He lifts his foot slightly so Sloth can

speak and kicks him hard in the groin.

"OK, ok!!!" says Sloth, writhing in pain, "You pathetic worm Sloth, keep your mouth shut!" Suicidus quickly make his way back to his cell, the way he came. Morning comes and Sloth demands to speak to Petrova. She arrives at his cell.

"What is it?" she asks nervously.

"I want to withdraw my statement. I'm not going to testify." says Sloth fearfully. Petrova looks at him and guesses immediately that there has been foul play. "Who's got to you Sloth? We'll sort it!"

"NO, NO, I mean it. Get me out of this apartment and take me back to the cells. I won't rat out my friends." Petrova is furious. She addresses the guards, "Take him to solitary, the dirtiest cell you can find!" "I'll make sure you regret this Sloth, hope it was worth it!" Petrova storms off angrily, shouting at the guards and demanding to know who was on duty during the night and to see the CCTV footage from the mobs prison wing. She observes Suicidus creeping about during the early hours.

Petrova meets up with Floss and Swallow to discuss the situation.

Floss suggests they present Suicidus with the video evidence they have to see what he says. It's admissible in court. Petrova and Floss interview Suicidus again.

"What's going on Suicidus? Sloth has withdrawn his statement and you were seen creeping around the prison and entering his apartment?" asks Petrova.

"Nothing to do with me!" Floss plays the video footage of Su creeping around the prison and his attack on Sloth, now he can't avoid the video evidence set before. He says nothing.

As Petrova goes out of the prison door Suicidus makes a run for it. He barges through the door sending Petrova flying into the guard. He runs head first at the barred window opposite his cell door and at that moment the super human strength of these creatures suddenly becomes apparent as he smashes through the window, spreads his wings and flies off into the dark. The guards take flight after Suicidus but he's too fast for them. He hides in an abandoned ship and then makes his way to the Aokigahara Forest in Japan at the base of Mount Fiji. Suicidus knows this forest like the back of his hand as he had a following here for years with people regularly coming her to end their lives. He hides away in the dense woodland.

Back on Alcatraz Island Petrova is checked over in the sick bay. The force of the shunt landed her with a broken rib and a sprained ankle, but her biggest injury is her pride and the disappointment at loosing such an important witness.

"We've still got the video evidence," Floss reassures Petrova. This will still stand up in court.

"Contact Archangel Michael and tell him what has happened and send out a search party to bring Su back. He must be located!" demands Petrova, determined to rectify the situation.

A messenger Angel approaches swallow and gives her a letter. It's from Teetotaller.

'Dear swallow,

How are you? I hope you're well. I just wanted to write and say how much I enjoyed the time we've spent together. I understand that our situation is risky, to say the least. Me being an angel and you being human, but I just got to tell you that the first time I saw you that day I was gob smacked by your beauty, your beautiful smile, your precious eyes that sparkle like diamonds when they catch the light. I enjoyed every single second of the time we spent together and I can't wait to see you again. I know you've got your problems and I've got mine but you're the first thing that comes into my mind when I wake up and the one I go to sleep dreaming about. I love you Swallow and I'm hopeful, hopeful that you and me can get together one day.

Love

Teetotaller

Swallow is over the moon that Teetotaller feels this way about her and is so hopeful that he will humanise.

Chapter 10

The Abyss

The abyss is the most evil, uninviting place left on earth. It houses Satan himself, plus all the demons and unbelievers. The unbelievers are sent to the level that characterises their most predominant sin when they were alive.

The abyss starts on the earth's surface and goes right down to its core. Its circumference is 1.5 kilometres. Its depth – nobody knows because nobody has ever come out to tell the tail.

The first level of the Abyss is for The Uninformed, who at the time of the return of Jesus had not, for whatever reason, been given the opportunity to commit their lives to him or hear the gospels. After the prohibition of Christianity many new born children grew up having not had the opportunity to hear or understand the truth let alone make a commitment. The first level of the Abyss starts on ground level and covers a five mile radius around the actual crater itself. The uninformed help the angels in the daily management and protection of the abyss and many are involved in naturalisation projects. In a thousand years when Satan and his demons are released they will be given the opportunity to decide what they believe and where they wish to reside. Heaven or Hell.

The next layer of the Abyss houses the Proud. Here the rich serve the poor. The slaves, those who never stood a chance of reaching a life boat on the Titanic. Those who starved to death whilst others ate gluttonously are served by those who were rich and proud in their lives on earth. Those who were never allowed to reach their full intellectual potential because of financial restraints are taught by the educationalists who educated the elite on earth.

Those who are thrown off the path to knowing Jesus because of their sexuality are appeased by those who boosted their own egos in unrepentant self righteousness.

Those who were exploited by the wealthy. Those unfortunates who were stripped of financial support so that politicians could falsely claim success in saving the economy, whilst ignoring the death toll caused by their dangerous policy making are served by the very politicians who stabbed them in the back. They sit on leather settees and have their feet and hands cleaned with sweet smelling oils by the very people who sentenced them to death. Stripped of their expensive clothes and jewellery. They must answer to the beck and call of the oppressed and exploited for a thousand years and beyond. Those Christians who started out in ministry for the Lord and ended up believing that they were more important than God himself are also here. It was pride that originally got Satan kicked out of heaven when he said that he would raise himself up above God.

The envious occupy the third level of the Abyss. Envy is the opposite of love because while love celebrates the good of another, envy seeks to destroy another in order to benefit oneself. This level is run by Cain, Abel's brother, who envied his brother's relationship with God and consequently murdered him. It consists also of thieves and adulterers who acted out of a desire to have what belonged to someone else. There are also many people who envied others for their achievements, looks and intelligence and took it away from them. They start their thousand years in the Abyss thinking that they have been given a prize. A beautiful partner, a home, a gift or something else that they value very highly. This prize is then taken away from them and given to someone else right under their noses. They must experience the pain of this loss for a thousand years whilst in the Abyss. They are led to believe that they may get it back but then they are let down right at the last minute.

The Gluttons occupy the fourth level of the Abyss. Those who ate food that is too luxurious, exotic, or costly have to live off dry bread alone. Those who ate too much food had to suffer as those who lived in famine on earth.

Those who idolised food by eating food that was too daintily or elaborately prepared were given nothing but bland rice. Those who ate too soon, or at an inappropriate time were only allowed to eat once a day and those who ate too eagerly were given rations. These punishments were to last a thousand years.

The unrepentant lustful occupied the fifth level of the Abyss. This includes those who lusted for knowledge, sex or power.

Those who lust for sex includes pornographers, prostitutes, pimps and adulterers alike and those who sexually exploited the young and vulnerable. Their punishment is to feel the pain of castration endlessly for a thousand years. Those who lusted for knowledge and power are tormented by their uselessness and powerlessness in the abyss.

The fifth level of the abyss is enormous as it covers a multitude of sins. This level is for the Angry. Here are found all the murderers, those who refused to forgive, the violent, those who took the Lord's name in vain, the war mongers, those who caused divisions amongst nations, the verbally abusive, the physically abusive, the wife beaters, the mockers, the scornful and the hateful. The terrorists and their despot leaders. Their punishment is burning in fire. The fire never dies down and neither does the pain.

The greedy occupy the next level of the abyss.

The 6th includes those who lusted after power, wealth and sex excessively and to the cost of others. On this level there are many government leaders and officials who withheld monetary and food aid from the poorest of the world's people. There were bankers who financial policies stole billions from vulnerable people who did not really understand finance. There are mill and factory owners who exploited their employees to line their own pockets. There are the directors of energy companies whose pricing policies made them billions in profit whilst driving the poorest families even further into debt.

There are gambling tycoons who enticed millions into addiction to line their own pockets with money they did not need. There were business owners whose companies were too greedy to protect the planet and consequently damaged the natural environment, killed millions of animals and damaged many innocent people's health. Their punishment is to wander a vast maze of emptiness, poverty, pollution, despair and hardship for a thousand years, learning how it feels to be on the receiving end of their own exploits.

This 7th level of the Abyss is occupied by the Slothful. This includes the unrepentant drinkers, drug takers, those who refused to work and those who exploited hard workers for financial gain. Their punishment is to hold up the foundations of the Abyss with their bare hands, for a thousand years.

The next three levels of the Abyss are for the demons only. With the exception of Level 8.

Level 8 is for the demons that were following orders. It is also the level for drug dealers. Their punishment is hell fire.

Level 9 is for the demons that gave out the orders. Their punishment is hell fire and torture.

The 10th level of the Abyss is for the demon leaders. Their punishment is hell fire and one thousand years of torment and torture from those they hurt.

The Eleventh level is for Satan only and can only be described in tongues incomprehensible by the human ear.

All said. The Abyss is not a good place to end up. The sad fact is that so many could have avoided it by coming to know Jesus Christ as Lord and

Saviour.

Chapter 11

Teetotaller Returns

Te arrives to learn that Suicidus has escaped from Alcatraz and that the court case is now only seven days from beginning. He goes to see Petrova.

"How is it going Miss Petrova?" asks Te observing the bandages she is wearing around her waist and on her ankle.

"The evidence we have collected has given us a very strong case against Abs and his crew. The problem is that Su has escaped after scaring Sloth into silence." replies Petrova glumly. "Te has you thought about humanising? You could clinch the case for the prosecution!" asks Petrova cautiously. Te hesitates...

"Do you understand the implications of what you are asking me to do?" answers Te calmly, "I've been an angel since...forever! Nobody feels more strongly than me about what Absinthe did to Maria and thousands more of my protégés but ultimately Abs and his crew are going to the Abyss, regardless of what level they go to, their final destination is the same. Is it worth it?"

"Is it worth it? Te this is not just about where they get dumped in the Abyss...this is about JUSTICE! Justice for those that Abs and his crew deceived, do you understand that? Abs claims that the humans chose to drink but they were totally unaware of the dynamics that were going on around them in the spiritual realms...they were deceived!" Te looks to understand what Petrova has just said to him.

"I'll tell you in the morning." Te replies touching Petrova's arm respectfully he departs.

Abs flies to the top of a mountainside and looks down on the new kingdom being built below. He observes the naturalisation process that continues 24/7 around the world. He flies over the new forests and lakes observing the beauty of the new kingdom and is awe struck by the sites he sees. Animals that have been extinct for years. Humans and wild beast walking alongside each other. Beautiful lush green countryside and a clear blue sky with fresh air. Air fresher than it's ever been since Eden.

Te remembers Eden. He flies over to the original garden where Adam and Eve fell from grace. Before he lands a messenger angel flies up next to him and gives him a letter.

Dear Te,

thanks for your beautiful letter. I honestly feel the same way if I'm honest and I too hope that one day we will be able to get together. I really loved the time we spent together that weekend. There's so much to sort out though and if you don't humanise it will never be possible. I love you too Teetotaller. Let's meet up soon.

Swallow

Te's heart jumps as he reads the good news from Swallow.

He sits a few yards from the tree of knowledge of good and evil. He thinks about his life, his jobs, about what he is and what he could be. He thinks about Swallow and how he would be able to have a relationship with her if he humanised.

As he sits there an elderly man comes wondering by. He sits on a log next to Te and greets him warmly,

"Hello Te", Te is surprised that this man knows his name. "Who are you?" asks Te.

"Just a shepherd... I was just checking that I've still got all my sheep. What's bothering you?"

"I've been asked to humanise so that I can testify in court against Absinthe and his cronies. I don't know what to do!"

"So you feel scared",

"I guess...I don't know what I would do as a human. I've always been an angel!"

"So you wonder how and where you would fit in as a human" "Yes, what would you do?"

"I don't have the answer my child. The answer is in your heart. Human or Angel you are part of the kingdom of God, loved and accepted for eternity. Nothing can ever change that...wings or hands will make no difference."

"Yes...and I guess justice for the deceived does matter, plus there's that girl Swallow"

The Sheperd smiles warmly "My child I think you've answered your own question."

"There's just the application to make and the operation to go through." sighs Abs, "I may not even be in time for the case."

"Do I take it that you have decided to humanise?" asks the elderly shepherd gently.

"YES! I will" replies Te excitedly. A few feet away from the tree of knowledge and light there is a crystal blue pool. The elderly man looks at Te and in a gentle but commanding voice say, "Te walk through that pool!" Te doesn't even question him. He walks towards the pool and cautiously enters it. He gets deeper and deeper into the water. As he comes out the other side he feels different, lighter...as he looks down he notices he has hands. Te looked behind him, his wings have gone. Te looks at the old Shepherd again and suddenly he realises who he has been talking to..."Oh my..." "God!" the old man finishes his exclamation for him. Te looks down sheepishly but the old man smiles and gently says, "Now go and bring justice for the deceived, don't worry about fitting in. Trust me! He smiles at Te and walks off into the forest.

The morning after, Te wakes up early and prepares to head to Alcatraz to see Petrova and show her the good news. He instinctively jumps out of the window expecting his wings to kick in and then remembers "Ooooh shi..." he hits the ground with a thud. Te picks himself up and brushes himself down, thanking his lucky stars that his body is the upgrade model. He feels a bit humiliated as a passing navigator asks him if he wants a lift somewhere.

"Yes please! Alcatraz" The navigator drops him off at the landing bay on Alcatraz and Te is full of ambivalence about his new body but determined to follow through with what the Lord told him.

Petrova meets him in the landing bay and is overwhelmed and delighted at the change.

"How! When! Who did..!" asks Petrova. "It's a long story", replies Te cheerfully.

Chapter 12

The Court Case Begins

The Day before the Case. The Courts of Justice.

The witnesses start to arrive for the case and they are shown to their apartments within the court complex. The apartments are usually heavily guarded but are even more so now with the underlying knowledge that Suicidus is out there somewhere and could attempt to get to the witnesses.

The Jury

The Jury for the case consists of six Angels – Cherubim, the second highest order. There are also six risen humans, chosen at random from the naturalisation projects.

The Jury are shown to a secure suite within the court building. This will be their home for the duration of the case. Unlike Juries in the old world order, this jury's job is not to judge the defendants guilty or innocent. That is God's job... The jury is there to praise God and pray for justice throughout the case.

In the Judge's box sits the highest Seraphim. This Angel is God's representative as the world is still too unclean for God to preside himself.

Petrova meets with the witnesses who have come forward to give evidence in the case. Te, Karl, Pedro, Helen, Albert, Mr and Mrs Birtwistle and Emma Harris. The main topic of conversation when she arrives seems to be Te's transformation into a human and she sees that Te looks a little uncomfortable at all the questions he is being bombarded with so she intervenes and calls the group to order.

"Lady and gentlemen!" Petrova brings the meeting to a start, "Thank you for coming and bless you for your courage in standing up for justice. As you know the case starts tomorrow."

"What's with all the security?" asks Karl.

"In cases like this there is always high security; however, we have suffered a minor setback which means that we've had to double our normal security arrangements."

Emma looks concerned, "Are we safe?"

"Yes! I assure you all that you are safe! Please don't worry about a thing." Petrova reassures them.

Johns meet with Absinthe and his crew.

John has so far resisted the temptation to go and retrieve the whisky that Abs told him about the other day.

He meets up with Absinthe and his crew in an interview room in the Courts of Justice. Absinthe and his friends are all wondering where Suicidus is. Sloth is not present.

"I hope you've come up with something good John because if our ship sinks we are going to take you down with it!" threatens Abs. John plays it cool but inside he is scared and the only thing he can really think about is the whisky.

"Gentlemen we are going to play it cool."

"Where are Sloth and Suicidus?" demands Desparus. "Su has escaped and sloth has retracted his statement so he's been thrown into solitary confinement." The gang laugh at what they consider to be good news. "Well this should make it a little more difficult for the prosecution. Shouldn't it John?" asks Absinthe. John agrees cautiously.

"Gentlemen let's cut to the chase! In half an hour I have a meeting with the DA. In that meeting I have to tell her how you all intend to plead. If you plead not guilty and are found guilty you will be sentenced to a lower level of the Abyss than if you come clean now. Do you all still wish to plead not guilty?"

"Yes John because you are going to get us off aren't you?! Threatens Absinthe.

"Well I'll do my best" replies John weakly and ends the meeting with the crew.

"Hey John don't forget about that little package I told you about!" taunts Abs. John leaves the room quickly and runs to the rest rooms. He violently kicks open a cubicle door and throws up in the toilet.

The anxiety and stress of the case is too much for him to bear already. He sits on the toilet with his head cupped in his hands and his mind drifts off to before the return of Jesus, before he made a commitment.....He was considered the best defence lawyer in town. Every win was celebrated with a night of drinking and celebrating in the 'The Chambers' a bar frequented by legal eagles. If any case was particularly stressful John had his hip flask full of whisky to see him through the long stressful days in court and a pocket full of mints to disguise the smell. This was common practice for many lawyers, doctor and other highly stressed professional in the city. After he made his commitment John tried to stop the drinking but then there was really so little time as his arrest and prosecution coincided with the rapture. Now he's back in the deep end again with no defence mechanism.

John composes himself, washes his face and heads off for the meeting with Petrova. Petrova has just finished her pre-trial meeting with the witnesses who have confirmed that they intend to testify as per their statements. John and Petrova meet in an interview room within the court.

"Hello John, Good to see you."

"and you Helga." replies John. They open their respective files and both look ready to do business.

"Are there going to be any changes John, in how your clients intend to plead?"

"None whatsoever." replies John in a matter of fact manner.

"You do know that the evidence we have against them is not just circumstantial. We have eye witnesses now",

"Yes they know and they still won't budge on their pleas." replies John.

"So be it!" smiles Petrova. Both attorneys stand and shake hands.

"May the best man win!" says Petrova.

"May the best man win!" repeats John "I hope you do!" he says to himself. Both lawyers go their separate ways.

Swallow sees Te in the corridor of the Courtrooms. She notices that the wings have gone and runs over to him to greet him. They hug each other warmly and he kisses her. The onlookers in the courthouse applaud and cheer as Swallow and Te are finally allowed to get together.

Day 1

The atmosphere in the courtroom is electric as everyone assembles for what will be the last ever court case in human history. Thousands of people line the streets outside to catch a glimpse of Absinthe and his crew as they are escorted into the Court.

The Jury have assembled and sit chatting amongst themselves. The witnesses are brought in by Petrova, Miles Hamilton, the attorney general and their team of legal clerks. Floss and Swallow sit behind the prosecution. The public and the press are kept right at the back of the courtroom.

Absinthe and his crew enter the courtroom and take their seats in the courtroom with their defence John.

The Seraphim enters from the front of the courtroom and sits in the judge's seat. The Bailiff exclaims, "All rise!" the Court is now in session. Judge Metatron the Seraphim presiding. Please be seated.

"Silence in court!" orders the Seraphim. The noise in the room descends to a deadly silence.

"Good morning, ladies and gentlemen. You have been selected as the jury in the matter of State versus Absinthe, Desparus, Metus, Culpus, Lustus, Suicidus and sloth.

Petrova address the Seraphim," Ready for the People, Your Honour." as does John ,"Ready for the defence, Your Honour ." "Will the clerk please swear in the jury?" ask Metatron.

The Clerk addresses the jury, "Will the jury please stand and raise your right hand? Do you swear that you will fairly pray for the case before this court, and that you will pray for the return of a true verdict according to the evidence and the instructions of the court, so help you, God? Please say "I do". The jury affirm that they will return a true verdict. "You may be seated."

Petrova stands up and addresses the Jury. "Your Honour and ladies and gentlemen of the jury: the defendants have been charged with Genocide and multiple war crimes against humanity, resisting arrest and psychological warfare. The evidence I present will prove to you that the defendants are guilty as charged and should therefore be placed in the penultimate level of the Abyss."

John stands up and addresses the Jury. "Your Honour and ladies and gentlemen of the jury: under the law my clients are presumed innocent until proven guilty. During this trial, you will hear no real evidence against my clients. You will come to know the truth: that they were simply fun loving demons who liked a drink and a laugh with humankind. Unfortunately humans couldn't always handle their liquor and chose, THEMSELVES! to drink too much. My clients therefore are not guilty and don't deserve the penultimate layer of the abyss.

"The Prosecution may call its first witness" announces the Seraphim. "The people call Helen Brown," says Petrova. Helen nervously takes the stand, accompanied by the bailiff. The clerk swears her in, "Please stand. Raise your right hand. Do you promise that the testimony you shall give in the case before this court shall be the truth, the whole truth, and nothing but the truth, so help you God?" Helen replies "I do", the clerks ushers her to sit down. Petrova addresses Helen. "Miss Brown, how old were you when you first met Absinthe?

"About seventeen I think" she replies

"and how would you describe your relationship with him when you first met?"

"He was great fun, as I said he went under a different name back then, called himself Jack, Jack Danyal. He kept me entertained for nights on end."

"When did your relationship life start to deteriorate through knowing Absinthe would you say Miss Brown?"

"His friends started to come round during the day. They started taunting me, bullying me."

"Are these 'friends' present here today Miss Brown?"

"Yes"

"For the benefit of the Judge and Jury Miss Brown could you please point them out?"

"There", pointing at Sloth, "the fat one." "Well the cheeky mare!" exclaims Sloth.

"For the record you are pointing to Sloth is that correct?"

"Yes"

"Any more miss Brown?"

"That one there....Desparus and that one...Culpus!"

"And why did they have such a negative effect on your life miss Brown?"

"Sloth used to come and tell me not to go to work. He would turn up in the morning and tell me it wasn't worth going out."

"Did he force you to stay home or did you choose to stay home?"

"He didn't force me but Desparus use to come and taunt me. He made me feel too depressed to go to work."

"Then what would happen?" asked Petrova,

"That one there Culpus. He would drop by usually around mid day or just after work had phoned me to ask me why I wasn't in. He used to bully me, push me around. He told me that all the shit in my life was my fault and that I was a bad person."

"Did you believe him?"

"Yes I did"

"Did you meet any more of absinthe's crew miss Brown?"

"Yeah, that one there...Metus"

"And how did he treat you?" asks Petrova.

"He used to scare me. He always told me that I was going to die."

"During a typical day how long would this torment go on for?"

"Until Absinthe came back and we started drinking again."

"Did Absinthe change towards the end miss brown?

"Yeah, he stopped defending me against his friends unless I drank so much."

"What happened on the night you died?"

"I'd lost my job. They would not stop the bullying, they kept going on and on at me night and day. I can't remember a lot about that night. I'd fallen outside and hurt my back, I could hardly walk. Another friend of theirs arrived; I'd never met this guy before."

"What did he say to you Helen?"

"He told me to just take some pain killers with a glass of whisky and I'd feel better. Absinthe agreed, said it would stop the pain. The last thing I remember is taking those pain killers."

"Do you recall the name of that friend Helen?"

"He was called Suicidus."

"Do you think what happened to you was your fault Helen?"

"They bullied me. Absinthe' was great at first but towards the end he was so demanding. Kept trying to get me to drink more and more before he would show me any affection."

"I have no further questions". Says Petrova.

"Does the defence wish to ask any questions"?

"Yes, Your Honour". John stands up to address Helen.

"Miss Brown, why did you let Absinthe's friends into your life if you hated them so much"?

"I don't know.....well I guess they came as a package. There were times when I didn't see too much of Absinthe and when I didn't see him they disappeared as well." John immediately regrets asking the question and moves on quickly.

"Miss Brown. You blame my Client Sloth for causing you to lose your job but ultimately you chose not to go into work. Is that not so?"

"Yes because Desparus made me feel so depressed and down!

"However you still chose not to go in" replies John.

"Miss Brown why would you choose to believe Culpus when he allegedly said that all the shit in your life was your own fault and that you were a bad person"?

"When you're told something over and over again most of the day you start to believe it. He only let up when absinthe got back".

"Finally Miss Brown you mentioned that Metus used to come round with Desparus. Surely you can't be trying to tell the jury that both of these fun loving creatures were out to get", laughs John, "one would surely think that you were paranoid"?

They worked as a team, when I look back and think about it. They were like clockwork.

"Thank you. I have no further questions", says John. John is not happy at how the first witness statement has turned out.

The Prosecution may call its next witness, says the Seraphim.

"The People call Pedro Escobar" shouts the Clerk.

Pedro is escorted to the witness box by the Bailiff. "Please stand. Raise your right hand. Do you promise that the testimony you shall give in the case before this court shall be the truth, the whole truth, and nothing but the truth, so help you God?" asks the Clerk.

"I do" replies Pedro.

"Please state your first and last name"

"Pedro Escobar"

Petrova starts. "Mr Escobar would you please tell the court how you came to Know Absinthe and his mob".

"I lost my wife to Absinthe and his cronies".

"When did Maria start drinking?"

Maria's drinking started when our son was born. Over the years it got worse and worse. She was deceived by Absinthe all of our married life and beyond. She looked terrible throughout the mornings and never felt better until she'd had her first drink when he turned up.

Towards the end of our marriage the drinking was nonstop. The minute she woke up she would be drinking again. One afternoon Maria had had a lot to drink, it was about 5pm. She was driving to the supermarket to get some shopping. She barely missed an oncoming lorry and ended up in a ditch. She lost her licence because of Absinthe. After that her mood got worse and worse. Desparus and Sloth were always around in the morning. Culpus was a regular visitor as well; he used to show up with Metus. They taunted her and Absinthe would turn up and comfort Maria, towards the end though he would make her drink so much before he would do anything for her.

"I have no further questions". Says Petrova.

"Does the defence wish to ask any questions"?

"Yes, Your Honour". John stands up to address Pedro.

"Surely the reason your wife was so down is because you walked out on her after eighteen years of marriage Mr Escobar"?

"She'd been down for years before I left her".

"As concerns the drinking Mr Escobar. Did Maria not make her own choice to drink like a fish?" Pedro gets angry with John, "SHE WAS BULLIED AND TORTURED BY THOSE THUGS FOR YEARS!"

"Calm down Mr Escobar or you'll be held in contempt!" warns the seraphim.

"Sorry your honour, lo siento" Pedro gets emotional. "Maria came to depend on Absinthe's affection to protect her from the rest of his dirty cronies".

"No further questions your honour". John sits down. John is starting to feel very anxious that the evidence is not going their way.

"The time is 3.30 ladies and gentlemen. Court is adjourned until 9am tomorrow morning" says the Seraphim.

The court begins to empty. John makes a hasty retreat back to hi quarter in the court building. Petrova, Swallow and Floss go off to discuss the day's proceedings.

John sits in his room at the little square table. He is taunted by the pressure of the case and can't get the case of liquor than Abs told him about out of his mind. "Maybe tomorrow will be a better day" he thinks to himself.

Petrova and her team are quite pleased with the day's proceedings. They feel that their defence was a bit weak, didn't make much effort really, but they are not complaining. It all seems to be going in their favour, at least for now anyway.

Back in their cells the demons talk amongst themselves.

"Hey Abs with friends like John we don't need enemies"! Says Desparus.

"Is that guy actually on our side?" asks sloth sarcastically.

"It might be a good idea if you have a little chat with John tomorrow you lot, Desparus, and Metus! Collar him before court in the morning and put him straight. He's got to get his finger out!" says Absinthe.

"OK boss" reply the demons.

09:00 AM The Courts of Justice.

The court is reassembling for the day's proceedings. The prosecution are busy discussing who will take the stand today.

John enters an interview room with Absinthe and his mob. The minute the door closes Desparus and Metus collar John. Culpus pins John in his seat and Desparus starts,

"You're going to feel shit all the way through this court case John if you don't start defending us properly!"

"If you end up in the abyss with us John it will be your fault!" says Culpus.

"We'll expose you and take you down with us John! Nobody knows about your relationship with Abs, do they?!"

"OK, OK We'll have a better day today. Come on guys!" John says fearfully.

The door opens and the demons are ordered into the courtroom.

The Seraphim enters from the front of the courtroom and sits in the judge's seat. The Bailiff exclaims, "All rise!" the Court is now in session. Judge Metatron the Seraphim presiding. Please be seated.

"Silence in court!" orders the Seraphim.

Unlike yesterday. A couple of people in the public gallery don't take the

Seraphim's order to be quiet as seriously as the day before and they are ordered out of the building.

Petrova addresses the Seraphim,

" Ready for the People, Your Honour." as does John,

"Ready for the defence, Your Honour."

"The Prosecution may call its next witness." says the Seraphim.

"The people call Mr and Mrs Birtwistle your honour" replies Petrova.

The elderly couple are shown to the witness stand by the bailiff.

The clerk swears them in, "Please stand. Raise your right hand. Do you promise that the testimony you shall give in the case before this court shall be the truth, the whole truth, and nothing but the truth, so help you God?" They reply "I do", the clerks ushers them to sit down.

Petrova begins. "Would you please tell the jury of your involvement with Absinthe please?"

"Our son Mark died. He was a passenger in a car driven by his friend Ben on the 4th of October 1985. There were five of them altogether in the vehicle at the time."

"OBJETCION YOUR HONOUR!" shouts John, "millions of people died in car crashes throughout the years but the jury can't be expected to believe that every accident was down to my clients!"

"Well if you would just let the witness finish their testimony please", replies the Seraphim.

"What happened exactly?"

"They'd been out drinking since lunch time that day. They'd been seen in the pub in Whalley drinking heavily from lunch time. They were coming back along the main road, going extremely fast and were all over the road. Ben, the driver, tried to overtake a vehicle in front of him, as he approached the village. He was so drunk that he didn't see the bus coming the other way. The force of crash tilted the bus on its side as Mark and his mates were sucked under the chassis and out the back of the back of the bus in pieces."

"Did any of them survive?

"Not one of them. The toxicologist report showed that Ben was three times the legal driving limit at the time of impact".

"Is this toxicologist report available for scrutiny your honour?" asks John.

The judge asks Petrova the same question. "Yes your honour", she passes the report to the jury. The jury take time to read the report, as does the Seraphim.

"Your honour, as tragic as this is I don't see what this has to do with my clients?" John complains.

"On the contrary, your honour. If the defence have no questions for Mr and Mrs Birtwistle I would like to call our next witness." adds Petrova sharply.

"Are there any further questions for the witnesses?"

"No, your honour", replies John.

Mr and Mrs Birtwistle sit down again. Petrova calls Albert to the stand.

The clerk swears him in, "Please stand. Raise your right hand. Do you promise that the testimony you shall give in the case before this court shall be the truth, the whole truth, and nothing but the truth, so help you God?" He replies "I do", the clerks ushers him to sit down.

"Will you please tell the Jury your full name" say the Clerk

"Albert William Tatlock"

"Mr Tatlock you were the landlord of the hare and Hounds public house in Whalley, Lancashire, England in October 1985. Is that correct?"

"Yes, it is your honour"

Petrova grins. "You may address me as Ma'am Mr Tatlock"

"Right ma'am"

"Mr Tatlock, would you please tell the jury about the events of the 4th of October 1985. The day of the accident.

Absinthe was already sat at the bar when they came in at about 11.30. As soon as Ben approached the bar he was right next to him, silly jokes, encouraging them to drink as much as they could."

"How long for?"

"Until about half past three. Absinthe kept egging them on, they got sillier and sillier as the drinks were downed."

"Mark and a couple of the other lads were talking about phoning a taxi"

"Did they?" asked Petrova.

"No, Absinthe kept telling Ben that he was the big man! He kept going on at Ben about not leaving his car outside the pub because it might get stolen and that he could drive home safely with his mates and there'd be no problem."

"What happened after the boys had gone?"

They had a party that night......as news of the accident got round they got rowdier and rowdier. Absinthe was boasting about how he set the driver up for the accident, 'hook line and sinker.'"

"Those were Absinthe's exact words were they Mr Tatlock?" asks Petrova.

"Yes, 'He fell for that hook line and sinker' he said ma'am."

"I have no further questions". Says Petrova.

"Does the defence wish to ask any questions"?

"Yes, Your Honour". John stands up to address Albert.

John stands to address Mr Tatlock.

"Mr Tatlock. How many people were in your public house that afternoon?"

"A handful. It wasn't busy"

"So you were perfectly aware of what was going on with these young men then?" asks John.

"Yes, they were getting rowdy."

"Mr Tatlock. What was your policy on serving alcohol to people who were intending to drive?

"Objection your honour! This case is about Absinthe's involvement in the death of the driver and his friends, not Mr Tatlock's bar policies." Petrova protests.

"But an intervention could have saved their lives!" adds John,

"Sustained... the defence may continue with this line of questioning", the Seraphim commands.

"As I was saying before I was interrupted...What was your policy on serving alcohol to people who were intending to drive?"

Albert looks worried..."There was no policy as such"

"Mr Tatlock...you have just told the jury that the boys were visibly drunk, they were talking about getting a taxi, but did not phone one. DID YOU HEAR BEN SAY THAT HE DID NOT WANT TO LEAVE HIS CAR OUTSIDE THE PUB?" demands John,

Albert hesitates. "Yes I did..."

"DID YOU SEE BEN WITH HIS CAR KEYS IN HIS HAND BEFORE HE LEFT THE BAR MR TATLOCK?"

Albert remains silent. "Remember you are under oath Mr Tatlock!"warns John. "I did."

The jury and the members of the public start to talk amongst themselves about this astounding revelation.

"You honour Mr Tatlock is not on trial here" Petrova pleads.

John comes right back at Petrova. "Be that as it may your honour! Mr Tatlock made no attempt to intervene!"

"Sustained, carry on" replies the Seraphim.

"So you made no attempt to stop Ben or encourage him to phone a taxi and you knew that he was going to drive that vehicle in an unfit state Mr Tatlock?"

"No I did not" replies Albert shamefully.

"I put it to you Mr Tatlock that my client was not responsible for the death of those boys, he was merely having fun. You could have intervened. At the very least you could have informed the police that he was driving over the limit. Ben made his own choices, as did the other boys who chose to get in that car with him. No further question your honour"

The court is in uproar as the tables turn and everyone is pointing their finger at the unscrupulous landlord.

"Court is adjourned for the day. We will reconvene at 9 am tomorrow." shouts the Seraphim.

Amid the uproar Petrova storms out of the court room angrily. If looks could kill Albert would be dead on the floor of the court room right now.

Absinthe and his cronies cheer at the day's success as they are led off back to their cells.

"Well done John!" shouts Absinthe. John smiles uncomfortably and doesn't hang around for idle chatter. He heads back to his room, not impressed by his own success. He detests Absinthe and he is starting to feel increasingly unhappy that he was chosen for this task.

The nights are long and boring during a court case, when you have to reside on court property.

"Down to the ground floor. Cross the main road. Take 2nd street South East and left to the remains of the Folger Elizabethan Theatre. Take the stairs down into the cellar and look for an old filing cabinet. Third draw down. Bells Finest, 5 bottles." John reads the instructions that Absinthe gave him over and over to himself again and again. "Not tonight!" John goes to bed.

Day 3

The court reconvenes for the day's proceedings. Albert is still the main topic of conversation in the courtroom as the jury and members of the public settle down.

The Seraphim enters from the front of the courtroom and sits in the judges seat. The Bailiff exclaims, "All rise!" the Court is now in session. Judge Metatron the Seraphim presiding. Please be seated.

Petrova addresses the Seraphim,

" Ready for the People, Your Honour." as does John,

"Ready for the defence, Your Honour."

"The Prosecution may call its next witness." says the Seraphim.

"The people call Emma Harris your honour" replies Petrova.

The young lady is shown to the witness stand by the bailiff.

The clerk swears her in, "Please stand. Raise your right hand. Do you promise that the testimony you shall give in the case before this court shall be the truth, the whole truth, and nothing but the truth, so help you God?" Emma replies "I do", the clerks ushers her to sit down. "Miss Harris will please tell the jury about your father Bill Harris and what you witnessed Absinthe and his gang do, as a child growing up"

"Yes my dad. Absinthe got into his life when I was about twelve. Up until then he was a great guy, He'd always suffered depression off and on and apparently his childhood wasn't great but generally he was fine. He was about thirty four when the drinking started. He began going to the pub a couple of nights a week for a drink or two. Then it started getting later and later for a while until my mum and him had a big argument about him never being in until late. After that he started drinking a lot at home. He would sit there with Absinthe and drink a couple of cans before dinner and then carry on drinking into the early hours. Usually until he fell asleep at his table. Absinthe used to encourage him to wind my mum up or me and my sisters. He'd start bullying us when he had had a lot to drink" Violensus was there that night. He egged my dad on to totally trash the kitchen and he hit my mum and threatened my older sister. Absinthe sat their roaring with laughter thinking it was hilarious.....My mum left for a while and took us with her to our Nan's. They sorted made up though and for a while there was no sign of Absinthe but Desparus and Metus were round more and more often. They kept taunting my dad and he became more and more miserable. They used to tell him that he couldn't manage without Absinthe.""

"You heard this?" asks Petrova.

"On many occasions" Emma replies. "Sloth started coming round telling my dad to stop in bed and skip looking for work. Desparus and Metus kept turning up and then Culpus as well. They would bully him during the day, especially after he lost his licence for drunk driving and then his job. Absinthe started to come earlier each day until eventually my dad was drinking at breakfast. One night they were all there partying. My dad was shouting at my mum and being abusive. He picked up a carving knife off the kitchen top and threatened me with it. My sister called the police from her phone in her bedroom. The police came and arrested him. He was sent to jail. My mother was in so much debt now because of my dad's drinking. The house got repossessed because my dad hadn't worked for twelve months. He came out of prison on bail but disappeared from his bail hostel. When they found him he was taken to hospital in a really bad state. His liver was packing in. He was yellow. He was then taken to a prison hospital near Liverpool. He died in hospital after about six weeks."

"I have no further questions". Says Petrova.

"Does the defence wish to ask any questions"?

"Yes, Your Honour". John stands up to address Emma.

"Miss Harris. Your father must have been a difficult man to live with. Drinking constantly, no job, history of depression. Did your mother shout at him a lot?"

"She did get very angry with him."

"Did she shout a lot Miss Harris?"

"Yes she did..."

"Miss Harris, your father was a weak willed man who had suffered depression all his life; I fail to see how you can blame my clients for his choices. I also imagine that your mother's incessant nagging didn't help matters either."

"HOW DARE YOU! My parents were happy until my dad met Absinthe in that damn pub. Slowly but surely absinthe made my dad dependent on him, no thanks to his bloody crony friends!"

"Miss Harris you will watch your tongue in my court room if you please. I know this must be hard for you but please watch your language." says the Seraphim.

"Sorry your honour." she replies.

"No further questions your honour." Johns sits down feeling sorry for Emma.

"Court is adjourned for lunch. We will reconvene in one hour." The court starts to vacate as empty stomachs start to tingle at the smell coming from the court cantine.

John leaves the courthouse, not really thinking about where he is going, he cross the main road and continues down the street opposite the court. As he walks down he sees the Folger Elizabethan theatre on his left. He suddenly realises where he is and the temptation that now stands right before him. He feels a hot flush coming on. He starts to perspire, his heart rate increases as he thinks, "Just the one and I'll be able to push my conscience aside and wipe the damn floor with the lot of them." He quickly turns away from the theatre and heads back to the court house, praying as he goes for protection and guidance.

Lunch time draws to an end and everyone makes their way back to the courtroom for the afternoon's proceedings.

The court reconvenes and Petrova is given the go ahead to call her next witness.

"The people call Teetotaller."

Teetotaller is shown to the witness stand by the bailiff.

The clerk swears him in, "Please stand. Raise your right hand. Do you promise that the testimony you shall give in the case before this court shall be the truth, the whole truth, and nothing but the truth, so help you God?"

Teetotaller replies "I do", the clerks ushers him to sit down.

John looks confused.

"Your honour would the Prosecution please confirm to the court that this witness is actually human and not an angel or part angel. I personally don't understand what earth is going on your honour!?"

"Miss Petrova?" asks the Seraphim

"This witness was an angel your honour but he made the personal choice to humanise for the purpose of giving evidence in this case."

"On whose authority Miss Petrova? Asks the Seraphim?"

"God's authority!" adds Teetotaller. The seraphim looks at Te and realises immediately that this is true and gives Petrova permission to proceed.

Petrova starts, "The night Maria Escobar died where you were?"

"In France",

"Why did you suddenly go to your protégée?"

"Absinthe and his crew had led Maria down an alley way in the student quarter. They were pushing her about, She was upset. I saw Violensus walk up behind her and push her really hard onto the floor. She smashed her head on a curb stone."

"Then what happened?" I saw the life drain out of Maria very quickly. Her soul departed within a couple of minutes the fall was so violent. I attacked Absinthe. His friends attacked me but I beat them off. The next thing I woke up in a prison cell at headquarters.

"Teetotaller will you please confirm to the jury that you DID witness Violensus murder Maria Escobar down that alley?"

"YES, he murdered her...Violensus."

"No further questions your honour." Petrova sits down.

"Does the defence wish to ask any questions"?

"Yes, Your Honour". John stands up to address Te.

"Teetotaller, on the night in question, you were in France at the time of the alleged murder, and you flew to the aid of your protégée as soon as you realised she was in danger. Is this correct?

"Yes."

"When you got there you must have been tired from travelling, what? Three, four hundred miles?"

"I was an angel. Angels don't get tired like humans."

"It must have been dark down that alley though? How do you know for certain that Violensus or anybody else pushed Maria? She was off her head on alcohol."

"I have perfect night vision."

"Your honour Angels can't lie as you well know" Petrova adds.

"Your honour the witness is no longer an angel and humans are perfectly capable of lying as we all know."

"Your honour at the time that this witness made his first statement he was an angel!"

"Sustained Miss Petrova." The judge addresses the jury, "Please take note ladies and gentlemen of the jury that Angels cannot lay and at the time that

Teetotaller made his first statement he was an angel, therefore his statement is taken as gospel truth".

The court again goes into uproar as fingers start to point and voices start to rise at Violensus.

"Silence in court!" orders the Seraphim.

The onlookers settle down again as the Seraphim re-establishes order in the courtroom.

"No further questions your honour." John steps down and returns to his seat.

"Well that's buggered it for sure! Petrova's got them for murder! Why am I even doing this? They deserve what they get!" John says to himself.

"The people call Karl Fenn" says Petrova.

Karl is shown to the witness stand by the bailiff.

The clerk swears him in, "Please stand. Raise your right hand. Do you promise that the testimony you shall give in the case before this court shall be the truth, the whole truth, and nothing but the truth, so help you God?" Karl replies "I do", the clerks ushers him to sit down.

"Mr Fenn. You are a retired drug and alcohol rehabilitation worker. Is this correct?"

"Yes it is"

"and you worked at this boarding house on Colne road in Burnley, Lancashire?"

"Yes ma'am. I worked there as a drug and alcohol rehabilitation worker for over twenty years before the return of Jesus."

"Mr Fenn would you please tell the jury about the residents of the boarding house?"

"All the residents were addicted to alcohol or drugs of one type or another. Many of them who were in there left in body bags. Many drowned in their own vomit or fell and hit their heads. Quite often they wouldn't be found for a few days. Desparus, Culpus and Metus use to badger all the residents 24/7. They were real bullies. Sloth used to make it easy for them to stay home and do nothing. He showed them how to get easy money. Absinthe didn't do much entertaining when he was here. He just brainwashed them into believing that they needed him and they'd listen and obey...otherwise Desparus would come on really hard and Metus would scare the life out of them."

"Exhibit One your honour shows this writing which was captured on a bedroom wall in the boarding house -

'Life is shit', 'I wish I were dead'

The images appear in the centre of the courtroom as a 3D holographic image.

"What about Suicidus Mr Fenn?"

"He'd visit about two or three time a year. See that hole up there in the ceiling," Karl points to the holographic image. "Exhibit two, for the record, your honour" adds Petrova.

"One guy ripped the plaster off the ceiling there and looped his belt round that exposed beam. He hung himself. Nobody found him for several days and that was only because the smell got so bad!"

"And Lustus Mr Fenn?"

"Oh yes, we got a lot of working girls in there. Lustus would bring dirty old men in off the streets for the girls so that they could score and feed their habits."

Petrova shows the jury exhibit three, the cracked tiles at the bottom of the stairs.

"There was one man who lost his sight because of the drinking. He used to walk around bumping into walls. Eventually Violensus tripped him up when he was trying to come down stairs. My co-worker found him dead here."

"So you think that Violensus pushed the blind man from the top of the stairs?"

"Yes."

"Did anyone see Violensus push him?"

"Not on this occasion, no."

"No further questions your honour." Petrova sits down.

"Does the defence wish to ask any questions"?

"Yes, Your Honour". John stands up to address Karl.

"Mr Fenn. You allege that my client Sloth taught the residents of the guest house to make easy money. I put it to the jury that my client was merely trying to teach the residents to be more enterprising.

"By stealing, begging and soliciting, I don't think so!"

John looks surprised at Karl's astute come back.

"You also allege that my client Violensus pushed this blind man from the top of the stairs but this is nothing more than idle gossip, is it not Mr Fenn? The man was unable to see where he was going and he spent his life inebriated. I suggest that this poor gentleman did not need Violensus as an enemy as he was his own worst enemy!"

"Look at the tiles at the bottom of the stairs. That was not just a fall. He was pushed"

"And you have forensic evidence from a professional to back this up do you Mr Fenn"

"...No."

"Then I put it to the jury that this blind man fell down the stairs because he could not see and he was pissed as a fart!"

The humans in the jury laugh at John's comment. All but one of the angels look disapproving at John, the other tries desperately to hide a smirk. Absinthe and his cronies roar with laughter

"MR SMITH! I will not tolerate that kind of language in my courtroom! Silence I say!" looking dagger eyed at the defendants who quickly quieten down again"

"I apologise your honour. I put it to the jury that this blind man fell down the stairs because he could not see and he was drunk."

"Do you have any further questions Mr Smith?"

"No, your honour."

Karl steps down from the witness stand.

"The time is 5.30 ladies and gentlemen. Court is adjourned until 9am tomorrow morning" says the Seraphim.

The court begins to empty.

The court reconvenes for the next day's proceedings.

The Seraphim enters from the front of the courtroom and sits in the judges seat. The Bailiff exclaims,

"All rise!" the Court is now in session. Judge Metatron the Seraphim presiding. Please be seated.

Petrova addresses the Seraphim,

" Ready for the People, Your Honour." as does John,

"Ready for the defence, Your Honour."

"The Prosecution may call its next witness." says the Seraphim.

"The people call expert witness Dr Alex Floss" replies Petrova.

Dr Floss is shown to the witness stand by the bailiff.

The clerk swears him in, "Please stand. Raise your right hand. Do you promise that the testimony you shall give in the case before this court shall be the truth, the whole truth, and nothing but the truth, so help you God?" Floss replies "I do", the clerks ushers him to sit down.

Petrova starts. "Dr Floss will you please tell the jury what you do?"

"I am a psychological profiler for the FBI. I have over thirty years experience for the Bureau."

Petrova passes copies of Floss's profile of Absinthe to the judge and jury.

The jury take their time to read the profile. After an hour or so Petrova addresses Dr Floss.

"Dr Floss, on top of the evidence that you have collated in this profile. How many lives were Absinthe and his cronies responsible for taking annually?"

"According to the World Health Organisation 2.5 Million Alcohol-Related Deaths Worldwide per year."

"What illnesses in particular did Absinthe use to kill his victims?

"Mental and behavioural disorders due to use of alcohol, degeneration of the nervous system due to alcohol , alcoholic polyneuropathy ,alcoholic cardiomyopathy, alcoholic gastritis, alcoholic liver disease, fibrosis and cirrhosis of liver , alcohol induced chronic pancreatitis , accidental poisoning by and exposure to alcohol ,intentional self-poisoning by and exposure to alcohol, but this was more su's domain and also poisoning by and exposure to alcohol with undetermined intent, amongst others."

"And when people attempted to stop drinking Dr Floss? What methods did Absinthe use to keep them hooked?"

"Withdrawal symptoms included nausea, sweating, restlessness, irritability, tremors, hallucinations, and convulsions. Sometimes he would cause seizures. Many even died trying to give up."

"In your professional opinion Dr. Floss how did Absinthe and his crew operate?"

"They paraded as legitimate and they had their fingers in lots of pies. Absinthe would start the con by charming his victim. He would entertain them with nights out or nights in and this would go on over time and he would look for the slightest signs of weakness, maybe problems from childhood or a bad relationship, maybe an inability to cope with certain things. He would then distract and comfort his victim. Once he had won their confidence he would introduce his friends to the victim but funny thing – his victims never liked his friends. The evidence from the cases we have heard about during this case is proof positive of this. They hated Desparus, Culpus, Metus terrified them, Sloth won their confidence then cost them their jobs Suicidus only ever showed up to deceive one into taking their life and Violensus either got people into trouble with the law or pushed his victims to their deaths. Absinthe would seem to protect his victims from his friends who would make themselves scarce when Absinthe returned. This was a scam, it was all planned. Towards the end Absinthe's crew were relentless and Absinthe became more and more demanding that they drink more and more to win his affection.

They were a professional team of con men and highly skilled assassins working under direct orders from Satan himself.

"Thank you Dr Floss. No further questions your honour."

"Does the defence wish to ask any questions"?

"No, Your Honour". John feels overwhelmed by the evidence that the prosecution have submitted and know in his heart of hearts that there is little point in trying to question the expert witnesses' evidence."

"Court is adjourned until Monday morning at 9am."

The Miners

After the first stressful week of the trial Gabriel invites Floss and Petrova to take a flying tour of the new earth and how it is changing shape from the old order we all once new.

The Angel navigators fist take them to the old city of Jerusalem. They are taken to the top of a large mountain where they witness an amazing site. They see thousands of angels digging new foundations on what used to be the city of Jerusalem. Now that the buildings and old infrastructure have all been thrown into the Abyss a fifteen hundred square mile trench is being dug out which one day will house the new Jerusalem.

The navigators then follow Gabriel to Florida, USA, to what remains of the NASA space station. Floss and Petrova are given space suits to wear. Once they are suited up the angels take them up out of the earth's atmosphere and up above the clouds into outer space.

Once above the clouds they are awe struck by what they see. First they are taken to the Planet Phoebe where the angels are busy mining Jasper for the foundations of the new Jerusalem. Then they are taken to Mercury where they are mining Sapphire. Then they fly around Venus where they are mining Agate. Then Mars where they are mining emerald. On Jupiter they are mining Onyx; on Saturn they are mining Ruby, on Uranus they are mining Chrysolite, on

Neptune they are mining Beryl, on Callisto they are extracting Topaz, on the planet Rhea they are extracting Turquoise, on Miranda they are mining Jacinth and finally on Triton they are mining Amethyst.

These millions of tons of precious minerals are taken into the clouds where even more angels are busy fabricating the twelve layers of the foundations of the new Jerusalem.

The navigators then take Petrova and Floss back to earth to where the Atlantic Ocean once was. Thousands of angels dig around a huge brilliant white object deeply embedded in the sea bed. Gabriel explains,

"This is one of the pearls that will eventually form one of the gates of the new Jerusalem. They are digging it out so that it can be taken up into the clouds and become part of the city's infrastructure."

The size of the pearl is inconceivable. Gabriel spends all weekend showing Floss and Petrova lots of wonderful sights.

Monday morning inevitably arrives and the court is preparing to reconvene after the weekend. John has been kept himself busy and managed to resist the bottles of whisky hidden in the theatre nearby.

As for the proceedings. All the witnesses have now given their statements and now it is time for the defendants to be cross examined.

There are even more hasty reporters than ever trying to cram into the court house, which now seems under capacity for the importance and symbolism of the case.

The Jury have assembled again and sit talking. The witnesses are brought in by Petrova, and her team of legal clerks. Floss and Swallow sit behind the prosecution. The public and the press are kept right at the back of the courtroom.

Absinthe and his crew enter and takes their seats in the courtroom with their defence John Smith.

The Seraphim enters from the front of the courtroom and sits in the judges seat. The Bailiff exclaims, "All rise!" the Court is now in session. Judge Metatron the Seraphim presiding. Please be seated. The noise in the room descends to a deadly silence.

Petrova address the Seraphim," Ready for the People, Your Honour." as does John ,"Ready for the defence, Your Honour ."

"The people call Desparus your honour."

Desparus stands up and is sworn in.

"Please stand. Raise your right hand. Do you promise that the testimony you shall give in the case before this court shall be the truth, the whole truth, and nothing but the truth, so help you God?" Desparus replies "I do", the clerks ushers him to sit down.

"Desparus. Helen Brown says that you used to taunt her and make her feel miserable when Absinthe was not there?"

"I did not, I've never met her."

Petrova addressed Helen, "Miss brown, is this the demon that used to come to your house and taunt you?"

"Yes it is."

"Do you still insist that you don't know her? Do you recognise this writing?" Floss turns on a holographic image of the graffiti that Swallow copied off the walls of the house. 'Life is shit', "that's your writing isn't it Desparus, found in the Burnley Boarding House?"

"No!"

"You were seen writing it for pity's sake! Mr Fenn did you see Desparus write this?"

"Karl stands, "yes I did Ma'am, I saw him give the pen to the occupant of that room and I heard Desparus order him to write it"

"Well Desparus?"

Desparus says nothing.

"Your silence says it all Desparus."

"Objection your honour that's a very leading statement."

"Sustained. Why doesn't he answer?"

Desparus looks down and says nothing.

"What about Maria Escobar Desparus?"

"What about her?"

You helped finish her off down that back alley didn't you? After taunting her all her life. Team work Desparus! That's what it was all about isn't it? You all worked as a team to break your victims down until the time came to go for the kill, if illness didn't get them first."

Desparus still remains silent.

"Do you want to say anything about Bill Harris, Desparus?"

"He was weak!"

"Oh, so an easy target for you eh? Not such a hard nut to crack!"

"No further questions your honour"

John stands up to address Desparus. He feels ill, he is stressed that everything is going against him yet so ambivalent he has been driven to feeling sick. He sits down.

"Do you wish to address the accused Mr Smith?" the Seraphim asks. John doesn't reply.

"Mr Smith, are you going to defend your client?"

"I'm not feeling well your honour."

"The defence is not feeling well. We will adjourn until tomorrow morning at 9 am." The court room empties and John returns to his room.

"That's it!" John says to himself. I'm sick to bloody death of this damn case. We can't win!" The image of the bottles of whisky in that cellar is engrained into John's mind. "I'll go for a walk," he tells himself.

John leaves the court building and crosses the road. He heads towards the derelict theatre. He stands, hands in his pockets outside the theatre. "I can win this case if I have a drink." He inches towards the theatre then steps back and turns around, sweat pouring off his brow, "What will happen to me though if I give in and I get found out?" John rethinks his next move. "Well I'll just go and have a look and see if they are a good year, just out of interest" he deludes himself. John heads down the stairs into the cellar, his heart pounding, sweat pouring off him. He experiences butterflies that he's not experienced since his first day at junior school. At the bottom of the creaky old stairs he pushes on the cellar door, it's stuck! It will not budge. John becomes more and more determined and pushes forcefully on the door. It eventually gives and he enters the cellar but it is pitch black, he cannot see a thing. He fumbles around in his pocket and finds an old box of matches; he takes them out and struggles to strike a match, his fingers trembling in expectation and excitement. The room suddenly becomes visible. The huge cellar is an oblong shaped room with tables scattered all around, on the tables there are piles and piles of costume dresses and suits of all different shapes and sizes. Around the edge of the room there are scores of old filing cabinets containing scripts and lines from different plays that have been held at the theatre over hundreds of years. John searches the cabinets for the bottles, struggling to keep the match lit. The match eventually burns right down and catches John's finger before it goes out,"OW!" John searches impatiently for the box of matches in his pocket, there is one match left. He strikes it carefully; aware that time is now of the essence he searches frantically for the bottles. Just as the match is about to go out he find them in the bottom draw of one of the cabinets, "Bingo!" he exclaims. The match goes out but John is not bothered. He has found his treasure. He carefully scoops the bottles up in his arms like porcelain dolls and fumbles his way through the dark back towards the door at the other end of the room. He trips on a box that has been left on the floor. He feels himself going but manages to get his balance back. He cautiously fumbles back to the door safely. He heads his way back up stairs and sits where the moonlight is shining through the theatre window.

"Hmm Black label! 1985. A good year." John says to himself. John looks longingly at the bottles. He opens one of them. He relishes the click as the metal links on the bottle tears away from the metal links on the lid. He slowly unscrews the lid and the smell, "oh the beautiful smell", fills his lungs. The butterflies in his stomach now start to dance a real merry dance in his stomach. He relishes the smell, a smell that has comforted him over and over again throughout the years. He fills the cap with the golden liquid, the strength of it tingles his nose. John puts the cap to his mouth and slowly swallows the liquid. John experiences the burning sensation as it descends his throat into his chest and down into his stomach. The blood immediately rushes to John's head as a feeling of relaxation and merriness hits him head on. All the tension and stress of the court case start to lighten. John takes a good swig from the bottle this time and then another. He sits peacefully on the floor of the theatre, his cares and frustrations now melting away into the night air.

The next two hours pass really quickly as John sits reflecting on the good old days when he won case after case. When he's down to half a bottle he staggers back to the court house, swaying from side to side. He hides the four remaining bottles in his room and sits at his table with the remaining half a bottle. He now feels confident and ruthless. Nothing will stop John winning this case now; he's on top of the world. He eventually goes to bed to sleep it off.

The morning after John wakes up feeling rough. His head is pounding and his stomach is churning after the nights drinking. He takes a swig of the whiskey and fills his little hip flask and goes straight to Alcatraz at about 7 am, way before the case is due to start. He goes to Fay to ask her to be an expert witness again.

"OK Andrea, you can give it your best shot."

"What do you want me to say? Anything to try and get Absinthe and his crew off the hook. I'll leave it to you."

"Right. When?"

"Today."

"ok and you'll get me a better place in the Abyss."

"Yes."

John goes to court with Andrea Fay. The court is preparing to start the day's proceedings. John goes to the toilet. He locks himself into a cubicle and shuts the door. He takes a good swing from the hip flask and then takes a handful of mints and eats them. He enters the courtroom, slightly glazy eyed but feeling much more confident than the previous day.

Absinthe and his crew enter the courtroom and take their seats with John.

The Seraphim enters from the front of the courtroom and sits in the judge's seat. The Bailiff exclaims, "All rise!" the Court is now in session. Judge Metatron the Seraphim presiding. Please be seated.

"Silence in court!" orders the Seraphim. Good morning, ladies and gentlemen. Are you feeling better Mr Smith?"

"Yes your honour, John says confidently.

"Ready for the People, Your Honour." as does John,

"Ready for the defence, Your Honour."

"The defence may call its next witness." says the Seraphim.

"The defence calls expert witness Andrea Fay your honour"

Fay stands up and is sworn in.

"Please stand. Raise your right hand. Do you both promise that the testimony you shall give in the case before this court shall be the truth, the whole truth, and nothing but the truth, so help you God?" Fay replies "I do", the clerk ushers them to sit down.

John starts," Mrs Andrea Chattox Fay will you please tell the court where you lived?"

"I lived in the Pendle forest Lancashire."

"and what was your occupation?"

"I was a child protection social worker."

"What experience did you have of working with people with drug and alcohol-Related illnesses?"

"We used to take their children off them."

"and in your professional opinion Mrs Fay. Where these people taunted and terrorised by my clients Absinthe and his colleagues?"

"Not that I'm aware of." replies Fay.

"What caused them to drink then Mrs Fay? In your professional opinion?"

"lack of self control. We always gave them a fair chance to sort themselves out but more often than not they would just keep taking their drugs or drink"

"So they always received a fair trial Mrs Fay?"

"Yes."

"Thank you, no further questions your honour."

Whilst Fay is giving her statement in court Swallow shows Petrova the court documents that Helen Brown gave her and lo and behold she is the same social worker that was involved in Helen's case. Swallow even has an invoice from Helens' builders showing that the date they attended to inspect her home the builders were there.

"Do you wish to address the expert witness Miss Petrova?" asks the Seraphim.

"Yes your honour. If I may ask for a ten minute recess in light of new evidence your honour?"

"Yes, you may." replies the Seraphim

After ten minutes Petrova is ready to cross examine Fay.

"Mrs Fay. You have taken the oath to tell the truth, the whole truth and nothing but the truth" Petrova clarifies this. "You claim that these drinkers lacked self control and that Absinthe and his crew did not scam them."

"yes that's correct. They were weak willed." replies Fay.

"You were Helen Brown's social worker is that correct?" Fay looks over at Helen and suddenly looks uncomfortable, "Yes I vaguely recall Helen yes."

"Good Mrs Fay because she remembers you! Please look at the court documents here Mrs Fay page 151 why did you attend Helen's house to assess it for suitability when you knew she had builders in at that time. Helen had told you that they were due to complete two days later yet you still went on that day and deliberately based yours assessment on that visit. Why Mrs Fay?"

"We had no time left before the court hearing."

"The court hearing was not for another two months."

"I don't recall there being builders there at the time. Helen was always drunk, she has probably got confused." replies Fay

"On the contrary, Helens drug lab reports show that she was clean at the time of the visit, furthermore she has an invoice here from her builders, a reputable firm. The dates show that they were working on the property when you attended to inspect it?"

"I don't remember."

"Convenient for you Miss Fay, however, the evidence speaks for itself. Helen Brown claims that on numerous occasions you gained her trust and then used it against her?"

"I'm not on trial her I volunteered for this!" barks Fay

"Very true Mrs Fay. You are currently on the fifth level of the Abyss. What do you stand to gain from doing this for the defence? Your record shows that you've never done anything for anyone other than yourself?"

The seething Fay remains silent and doesn't comment.

"What about the other 29 discrepancies that are highlighted here? Were you in cahoots with her solicitor Mrs Fay? Her litigation friend's final statement was brushed under the carpet, as was her litigation friend's."

"I have no further comments."

"I BET YOU DON'T MISS FAY! Where did her child go?"

"She was put into a children's home."

"Yes, she was, and later abused by the carers that were supposed to be a better option than HER OWN MOTHER! You were working with Lustus, Desparus, Culpus, Metus and Absinthe weren't you Mrs Fay?"

Fay remains silent

What support did Helen Brown get after she lost her child?

"She was offered counselling."

"And the counsellors didn't have enough on their plates thanks to Absinthe's mob, without you creating more work for them? Work that was unnecessary

Petrova stands up angrily. "Your honour in light of the discrepancies that have been highlighted here I request that this woman's evidence be flagged as untrustworthy and incredible. There is a whole separate case her that needs to be referred to the courts of justice for trial after this case has finished your honour."

The members of the public and the press become very vocal at this request. The bailiffs try to restore order.

"Sustained, Silence in court!" demands the Seraphim.

"The defence calls Desparus and Helen brown your Honour."

Desparus and Helen Brown stand up and are sworn in.

"Please stand. Raise your right hand. Do you both promise that the testimony you shall give in the case before this court shall be the truth, the whole truth, and nothing but the truth, so help you God?" Desparus and Helen reply "I do", the clerk ushers them to sit down.

"Miss Brown. You were a keen drinker when you were younger were you not?"

"Yes I was."

"and you chose to continue drinking even though the alcohol was having a bad affect on you and ended up costing you your job?"

"It was Desparus Metus and Culpus that terrified me and tortured me night and day."

"How was your childhood Miss Brown?"

"It was OK."

"Any problems?"

"My dad was a drinker"

"Your dad was a drinker! Well well. So surely you cannot blame my client Desparus for your bad drinking habits Miss Brown when your addiction was obviously genetic?"

"But they were there all the time from about two years of first meeting Absinthe and they never left until he arrived and in the end they were all there together."

"I put it to the jury that this is NOT the case. Miss brown's drinking was caused by a genetic disposition to alcohol-Related illness. No further questions your honour."

The jury talk amongst themselves. The Seraphim calls for silence in the court room.

"The people call Metus your honour" Metus is sworn in and sits down.

"Metus! Latin for fear. You know Helen Brown do you not, and Bill Harris and Maria Escobar?"

"No"

"How can you deny the evidence that has been presented to this court?!"

"No comment!"

"The defendant is refusing to comply with these court proceedings. I take this as an admission of guilt. No further questions your honour."

John feels like he has just been kicked in the nether regions as Metus' refusal to answer any questions throws their case even further into doubt.

"Court is adjourned for lunch" announces the Seraphim.

John meets with Absinthe and his crew in one of the court interview rooms during the lunch break.

"What the hell are you playing at Metus? You've nearly just blown the whole bloody case!"

Metus flares up and pins John against the wall but Absinthe and Culpus pull him off.

"Steady on Metus. Don't kill our only chance of a reprieve."

"John you are doing your best. We can't ask any more than that of you...and I see you have taken me up on my offer!" Absinthe winks at John.

"Well, lets just hope that it doesn't all go pear shaped" replies John and storms out of the interview room heading for the toilet.

He again locks himself into a cubicle and downs the remainder of the hip flask. Over the next four days Culpus and Violensus are grilled about their parts in the cases that were brought before the court. Both of them, like Metus, refuse to be honest with the prosecution and take John's case from bad to worse.

Furthermore, now that the whiskey has all gone Metus, Culpus, Violensus and Desparus are on John's case 24/7 just like they used to be but worse than ever.

"You're going to lose this case", says Metus.

"It'll be your fault if we lose John!"

"I'll finish you off if we end up worse off because of you!" says Violensus.

John has now finished his last bottle of Whiskey and he is feeling the effects of withdrawal.

On the penultimate day of the trial Absinthe has been questioned by Petrova and like his cronies, has refused to say anything of any value in his defence.

During the lunch break of the final day John heads for the old theatre again, in the hope that maybe Absinthe left another bottle lying around somewhere in the cellar. As he enters the grounds of the abandoned theatre he hears a voice behind him. "Hello John, I said we'd meet again."He recognises the voice immediately and is suddenly filled with remorse and guilt as he turns around.

"Hello Reverend. What are you doing here?"

"What are you doing here John?" asks the preacher calmly. "I'm just relaxing before the end of the case."

"John I know about the whiskey, the bullying. I know that Absinthe forced you to disclose who had grassed on them and then sent Suicidus to shut him up."

John collapses onto his knees in tears. The old preacher kneels next to John and prays for him with his hand on his back and suddenly the fear, the depression and the anxiety all lift and disappear. Back in the cells Absinthe and his cronies are suddenly filled with a chilling fear as they realise that something has gone dreadfully wrong. They all feel that their powers to harass and terrify John have been reduced to zero.

"The Seraphim has asked me to tell you that you are off the case, as of this minute. You are to go back to the court and speak to Petrova."

"OK, OK I will say John", relieved that it is all over, well nearly.

The court reconvenes after lunch and ever body notices John's absence immediately.

"Mr Smith has been called away and is unable to continue with the defence of this case. His deputy Mr Lewis will act for the defence during the remainder of the proceedings."

"The people would like to call a last minute witness your honour"

"Yes Miss Petrova."

"The people call John Smith your honour."

The court goes into absolute uproar. Absinthe and his crew have to be restrained by the largest guardian angels to stop them tearing John to shreds.

"SILENCE IN COURT!" shouts the Seraphim. The bailiffs arrest the rowdiest of the trouble makers and take them to the cells.

John is brought to the witness stand protected by two guardian angels.

John Smith stands up and is sworn in.

"Please stand. Raise your right hand. Do you promise that the testimony you shall give in the case before this court shall be the truth, the whole truth, and nothing but the truth, so help you God?" John replies "I do", the clerk ushers him to sit down.

"Mr Smith. Please tell the court how you know Absinthe and why you failed to make your relationship with him known to the court?"

"I first met absinthe at university. I was always out with my friends down at the student union. Absinthe was, as described, a great entertainer. I can remember some amazing nights out with him and my friends. "

"How did your relationship with him progress Mr Smith?"

"After law School and my legal practice course my first job was very stressful, working as a junior for the assistant DA's office in Boston. Everybody else new Absinthe and meeting up with him became a way of life. I then got married, had children, got a better job with a big law firm.

"Did the drinking become a problem?"

"On reflection it was a problem that was never discussed. It was a way of life. Even my wife drank a lot at all the social gatherings that she went to. Filling your hip flask at the beginning of the day was common practice, just like putting your bread in the toaster."

"So in your case where do Desparus, Metus and Culpus fit in? "

"If I didn't keep topping up with my hip flask throughout the day, Metus and Desparus would start niggling, then Culpus would start if the case started to go bad."

"Why did you not tell the court about your previous relationship with Absinthe and his crew?"

"Pride, I guess. I wanted to come out on top and finish my career on earth with a glowing record. What's more they threatened me. Violensus threatened to finish me off if I didn't win the case for them."

"Did Absinthe blackmail you to tell him who had grassed on him?"

"Yes he did."

"What did you tell him?"

"I told Absinthe that Sloth had grassed on them."

"Did you tell Absinthe where Sloth had been taken to?"

"yes, I did"

"So you knew full well throughout the whole of this case that Suicidus had threatened Sloth to keep quiet?"

"Yes, I did."

"Where has he gone?"

"I don't know."

"Mr Smith you are under oath. Where is he?"

"I do not know. How would I. He burst through the window. He didn't pop back to tell me where he was going and he didn't send me a post card."

The jury and the members of the public laugh at John's sense of humour in the face of adversity. Even the Seraphim and Petrova manage a smirk at his witty comment.

"OK, Mr Smith. You drank five bottles of whiskey throughout this case that Absinthe told you about?"

"I did."

"So Absinthe planted the seed in your head and the pressure of the case led you to give in to the temptation?"

"Yes"

"How much involvement did Desparus, Metus and Culpus have in the pressure you were under?"

"Most of it?"

"Is Mrs Fay a bonafide witness or did she lie?"

"She lied. She made up everything. She knows Absinthe and his crew because she relied on them constantly so that her victims would back slide and give them justification to snatch their children."

"Thank you Mr Smith, for telling the truth. No further questions your honour."

"Ladies and gentlemen of the jury, I am now going to read to you the law that you must follow in deciding this case. To prove the crime charged against the defendants, the prosecution must prove three things to you:

First, that the defendants did work as a team to destroy their victims; Second, that they are guilty of Genocide and multiple war crimes against humanity; and

Third that they resisted arrest and are guilty of psychological warfare. If each of you believes that the prosecution proved all three of these things beyond a reasonable doubt, then you should find the defendants guilty. But if you believe the prosecution did not prove any one of these things beyond a reasonable doubt, then you must find the defendants not guilty. Proof beyond a reasonable doubt does not mean beyond all possible doubt. It means that you must consider all of the evidence and that you are very sure that the charges are true. Are you ready with final arguments?"

"Yes, Your Honour." says Petrova,

"Yes, Your Honour." says Mr Lewis,

Petrova stands up and faces the jury. Absinthe and his crew escaped capture when Jesus returned and hid in an abandoned pub in Blackpool, Lancashire.

An operation to capture them, led by Teetotaller and a group of bounty hunter from the Cheshire regiment was successful.

During the operation Teetotaller sustained injuries to his chest from a bar stool that Absinthe through at him during the struggle

Also during the struggle Culpus found an old fire arm and shot Justicius in the stomach which resulted in minor injuries for him that would for the record have resulted in serious injuries for a human being. Justicius remained in hospital for two weeks after this incident.

On capture Absinthe and his crew were taken to Alcatraz island secure prison facility.

They were appointed John Smith as defence Attorney for the duration of this case.

Two junior bounty hunters were also seriously injured during the operation, by Violensus, who through them out of one of the pub windows. One of them sustained a broken wing and is still in hospital. The other suffered a fractured skull due to the force of the impact, which was so severe it left a hole in the tarmac outside.

In terms of actual war crimes against humanity. Before the return of Jesus Absinthe caused nearly 4 % of deaths worldwide, more than AIDS, TB or Violensus, according to The World Health Organization. Rising incomes caused an increase in drinking in heavily populated countries in Africa and Asia, including India and South Africa, and binge drinking was a problem in many developed countries according to the United Nations agency

Yet alcohol control policies were weak and remained a low priority for most governments despite Absinthe's heavy toll on society from road accidents, Violensus, disease, child neglect and Sloth. Approximately 2.5 million people died each year from alcohol related causes. 'The Global Status Report on Alcohol and Health.' stated that the harmful use of alcohol was especially fatal for younger age groups and Absinthe was the world's leading risk factor for death among males aged fifteen to fifty nine.

In Russia and the Commonwealth of Independent States (CIS), every fifth death was due to harmful drinking.

Binge drinking, which often led to risky behaviour, was now prevalent in Brazil, Kazakhstan, Mexico, Russia, South Africa and Ukraine and the United Kingdom, and rose elsewhere.

"Worldwide, about 11 percent of drinkers had weekly heavy episodic drinking occasions, with men outnumbered women by four to one? Men consistently engaged in hazardous drinking at much higher levels than women in all regions," the report said.

Health ministers from the 193 member states agreed to try to curb binge drinking and other growing forms of excessive alcohol use through higher taxes on alcoholic drinks and tighter marketing restrictions. This merely led to increased profits for Absinthe. Absinthe was a factor in 60 types of diseases and injuries.

There is physical evidence linking Absinthe to liver disease, epilepsy, poisonings, road traffic accidents, violence, and several types of cancer, including cancers of the colorectum, breast, larynx and liver.

There was actual evidence of a link between drinking and breast cancer.

Alcohol consumption rates varied greatly, from high levels in developed countries, to the lowest in North Africa, sub-Saharan Africa, and southern Asia, whose large Muslim populations often abstained from drinking.

Homemade or illegally produced alcohol accounted for nearly 30 % of total worldwide consumption. Some of it was toxic. In France and other European countries with high levels of consumption, binge drinking was rather low, suggesting more regular but moderate drinking patterns.

It has been proved beyond reasonable doubt that Absinthe and his crew worked as a team to reap psychological warfare on those who were susceptible to alcohol.

Absinthe the comforter and entertainer would woo his victims to trust him and once a dependency had been established he would release his pack of wild dogs on them – Metus, Culpus, Desparus, Sloth and Lustus would pick away at the very seams of their sanity driving the victim more and more into Absinthe's grip. Absinthe would then start to withdraw his affection from the victim unless they drank more and more and this inevitably led to death of one form or another. Metus, Culpus, Desparus, Sloth and Lustus also worked with Cocainas and Heroinas whose tactics were equally destructive. Suicidus, who we will discuss in more detail soon, was an assassin who worked directly under Satan and freelanced for Absinthe and Cocainas.

Metus, demon of fear, terrified Helen Brown, Maria Escobar, Bill Harris and his family and millions more besides. A deliberate, cold, brutal and calculated joint attack on the minds of humankind / the unaware. Metus used the notion of impending doom to terrify his victims and his catch phrase was "What if....?" with this.....he could put terrifying ideas into the heads of his victims. Metus was a master brainwasher. If he could get his victim to believe him he could convince them to die. He did this in a small village in Africa. He brainwashed the villagers into believing that if they were kicked out of the village they would die. Many did die...because they believed Metus and hence their vital organs shut down....and they died.

Desparus, alias "Depression", "Anxiety" "Stress", "worry" and many more was apt at lowering a victims mood. He was so expert in his job that he could render his victim paralysed if he wanted to...and quite often he did. He would bring them down so low that the only way back up was to reach out for Absinthe or Heroinas or Cocainas. He used brutal physical pain such as bodily aching, confusion, headaches, feeling choked up and upset etc., to control his victims. He would adopt a slightly different tactic with some victims, taking them on a lifelong roller coaster ride of ups and downs.

Culpus used conscience to plague his victims. He was the Accuser. He would point out every bad thing that the victim had done. He worked very closely with Fay and those like her. Picking out the bad and not acknowledging the good.

Responsible for three world wars and many smaller ones besides such as Vietnam, two Iraq wars, the war against terror in Afghanistan and many others. Violensus, demon of violence, was only involved part time with Absinthe and his crew, however, that involvement was still catastrophic. He was responsible for all domestic violence, pub brawls, murders, muggings, anger and factions throughout the world. He is the enemy of love. He was a Bishop in a major world religion that used him to brainwash its followers and keep them in their place. He was constantly underpinned by Metus. Who gave their victims a reason to flare up in anger?

There is, ladies and gentlemen of the jury, actual physical evidence that Violensus pushed Maria Escobar over and murdered her. An Angel cannot lie. It is not possible. You must therefore take the evidence by Teetotaller as gospel truth.

Violensus also tried to kill the two junior bounty hunters who were trying to capture him.

Lustus was a Freelance member of Absinthe's mob. He had his own rackets in prostitution and pornography but the evidence shows that he worked alongside Absinthe on many occasions.

Sloth led his victims into idleness and destroyed their self worth. This opened the door for Culpus and Desparus to attack, followed by Metus who would then stick the knife in.

Suicidus took approximately two hundred thousand lives per year throughout the one hundred and seven countries of the world. The evidence suggests that he finished off Helen Brown by encouraging her to take pain killers with such a high blood – alcohol content.

He threatened Sloth and consequently he has said nothing throughout this trial. He escaped from prison, seriously injuring myself and a prison guard.

Absinthe and his mob used John Smith's pride to lead him back into drinking and used the very tactics that have landed them here on trial on their own defence lawyer! However........as you haves seen members of the jury.......truth has prevailed! Justice has been done!

Andrea Fay worked closely with Metus and wilfully agreed to lie in court.

I put it to you members of the jury that Absinthe and his mob are guilty on all charges. The Human Race had free will, granted, but Absinthe's victims were victims of a complex and well thought out scam to lead them into addiction and take their free will away from them. This concludes the prosecution's final argument."

The court cheers at Petrova's outstanding delivery of her final argument. The court quietens down and Mr Lewis stands to address the jury.

"In light of the turn of events in this court room today and the evidence presented to the jury I have nothing further to say."

Absinthe and his crew try to break free from the guardians to attack Mr Lewis but they are restrained and made to sit down.

"The jury will now leave to pray on the final verdict" says the Seraphim. Court is adjourned.

John is taken off to Alcatraz and put in a prison cell. He must wait to see what his punishment will be for perverting the course of Justice.

Andrew Fay is sent straight back to the Abyss and not given any respite for her so called expert witness statement.

The jury are out for twelve hours. Petrova, Gabriel, Floss and the rest of the prosecution wait expectantly in the court room. Eventually the court is brought back into session.

The Seraphim addresses the spokesman for the jury.

"Have the jury reached a verdict."

"We have a verdict to deliver your honour", replies the spokesman.

"How do you find the defendants – guilty or not guilty?"

"We FIND Absinthe, on charges of resisting arrest, Genocide, multiple war crimes against humanity and psychological warfare.....guilty on all charges.

We FIND Desparus, on charges of resisting arrest, Genocide, multiple war crimes against humanity and psychological warfare.....guilty on all charges. We FIND Metus, on charges of resisting arrest, Genocide, multiple war crimes against humanity and psychological warfare.....guilty on all charges. We FIND Culpus, on charges of resisting arrest, Genocide, multiple war crimes against humanity and psychological warfare.....guilty on all charges. We FIND Metus, on charges of resisting arrest, Genocide, multiple war crimes against humanity and psychological warfare.....guilty on all charges. We FIND Suicidus, on charges of resisting arrest, Genocide, multiple war crimes against humanity and psychological warfare.....guilty on all charges. We FIND Sloth, on charges of resisting arrest, Genocide, multiple war crimes against humanity and psychological warfare.....guilty on all charges and We FIND Lustus, on charges of resisting arrest, Genocide, multiple war crimes against humanity and psychological warfare.....guilty of all charges resisting arrest, multiple war crimes against humanity and psychological warfare".

"The court is in uproar as the crowds try to attack the defendants. The guardian angels force the crowds back. Missiles are thrown at them from the back of the room. A relative that lost a loved one pulls an empty bottle of Vodka out of her shopping bag and launches it at Absinthe. The bottle smashes in Absinthe's face. He covers his face and falls over in pain, hitting his head, blood flying everywhere. The guardians quickly escort them out of the court room and the crowds are dispersed.

The Seraphim finds himself addressing the jury and a few remaining members of the public that weren't misbehaving.

"Court is adjourned for sentencing. We will resume at 9AM Monday."

Swallow and Te take advantage of the break to spend some time together.

"I'm so pleased that you've humanised. How did you manage to apply so quickly?"

"Oh, let's just say it was God's will."

"And now? Us? Smiles Swallow. "Definitely!" replies Te.

The Sentencing.

The atmosphere in the courtrooms is very solemn as the court reconvenes. Absinthe and his crew are brought back in to the dock.

The Seraphim enters from the front of the courtroom and sits in the judges seat. The Bailiff exclaims, "All rise!" the Court is now in session. Judge Metatron the Seraphim presiding. Please be seated.

Metatron start to speak, "In the matter of State versus Absinthe, Desparus, Metus, Culpus, Lustus, Suicidus and sloth. I have been instructed by the Lord to pass the following sentences in respect of which levels of the Abyss you are to occupy and what you will do there." Metatron looks slightly squeamish at the orders he has been given.

"Absinthe you are sentenced to level 10 of the Abyss for one thousand years. There you will be tortured by your own victims. Desparus you also are sentenced to level 10 of the Abyss. There you will suffer every depression ever suffered by every human, daily for one thousand years. Metus you also are sentenced to level 10 of the Abyss. There you will suffer every fear ever suffered by every human, daily for one thousand years. Culpus, you also are sentenced to level 10 of the Abyss. There you will be blamed for every guilty thought you ever inflicted on the drinkers and the drug takers, for a thousand years. Lustus you are sentenced to level 9 of the Abyss. There you will suffer the pain of castration, daily for one thousand years. **Suicidus in his absence is sentenced to Level 10 of the Abyss. Send the guardians out to locate and capture him. There he will spend a thousand years repeatedly jumping into level 11. Sloth, you are sentenced to level 9 of the Abyss. There you will hold up the eight levels of the Abyss above you for a thousand years.**

Andrea Fay you are to be tried for perverting the course of Justice. Your colleagues in the Abyss will also be investigated.

John Smith you have perverted the course of justice in this case. Whilst you are saved and no sin can change your right to remain in the kingdom. You will spend the next hundred years on Level 1 of the Abyss and then be returned to the kingdom.

Aokigahara Forest in Japan at the base of Mount Fiji.

Suicidus is dreaming in his sleep. He is back in Nelson, Lancashire in 2012......Tom stands looking down from the top floor of the multi storey car park. The weather is dull and cold, it is drizzling.

"Come on Tom, think about it! What's left to live for? Desparus has already made it quite clear. They've repossessed you car, your house, they've stopped your benefits, because chronic Arthritis is not a good enough excuse not to work nowadays! Just jump and it will all be over before you know it!" says Suicidus.

Tom developed Arthritis in 2007. On some days it was so bad that it took him forty five minutes to get from the bedroom to the bathroom, quite often he would soil his pants in the process. The new government however, were determined to cut unemployment to boost their ratings so instead of creating new jobs and boosting the economy that way, they took seriously ill people off disability benefit and stuck them on job seeking allowance. It would take Tom three hours to get to the job centre to sign on. When his appointment was at 9 am he had to get up at 4.40 in the morning to leave at 7am to get there for nine. It would then take him the same amount of time to get home.

If he was late he didn't get any money that week. John had just missed for the third time and had been told that his benefit was now to be stopped.

The government's position was that Sloth was causing havoc throughout the country and had convinced the previous government to make things too easy for people who in all honesty just could not be bothered to work because Sloth had brainwashed them. They claimed that this was costing the government billions.

When they were honest with themselves though, they new deep down that they were depressed and bored being stuck in all day with nothing to do and as the age old saying goes, "Idle hands make light work for the devil" how much truth there was in this- Absinthe very often found an opening in these situations.

Tom looked down at the passing vehicles.

"Just put one leg over to start with Tom, that's it, take your time... now the other" persuaded Suicidus. Tom stand on the other side of the railings five floors above the car park.

"Just let go and lean forward and it's game over Pal"

Tom falls to the ground toppling over as he goes. He hits the pavement head first at 40 miles per hour. A bus full of school children stuck in traffic by the car park witness the fall and start to scream as blood gushes from the dead man's body.

Suicidus suddenly wakes up to the noise of trees being ripped from the earth and carried away. He suddenly looks up to see a huge angel with ten heads standing above him. The angel grabs Suicidus and takes him to the Abyss where he is thrown in and sent down to the penultimate level.

The First Born of the Millennium

Just so you don't get confused, 'The Millennium' is not the year 2000 but the thousand years that Satan and his demons are locked away in the abyss.

From deep within the dense beautiful forests of the new kingdom of Jesus a baby cries out its first cry. Her parents Te and Swallow look in awe at their beautiful new born baby. They have been married by Jesus himself and Te has been made a General in the new army that has been created to restore peace, law and order to the new kingdom.

Naturalisation continues throughout the world. All the buildings, roads, bridges, every structure created by man is broken up piece by piece and thrown into the Abyss.

The saved enjoy their new bodies. They work hard and enjoy their new way of life.

There is urgency though to meet the needs of those who have been left stranded in parts of the world where naturalisation hasn't started yet. Relief in the form of food and clean drinking water is taken to them and part of Te's job is to ensure that unlike in the old world order, this aid does actually get to them.

As more and more children are born and start to grow up new schools are created. The schools are not made of concrete, bricks and mortar but people. The curriculum in these new schools is about teaching about their creator and ruler Jesus, language, social skills, history of the world and how and why they exist as they exist now plus the dangers of evil and free will.

Eventually naturalisation is completed and the whole world is now free of the dross that once was. The Ozone layer has been completely mended and now the weather throughout the world can function naturally again without God's intervention. There is no rain. The plants and the trees grow naturally.

There is love, peace and harmony throughout the world like nobody has ever experienced before. There is one language, as before the tower of Babel.

Nobody gets any older in the new world order, except the children of course who grow up to be fine young men and women. The population of the world starts to increase again more and more rapidly.

New churches are created to house everybody. Everybody goes to worship the Lord three times a day because He is the centre of their lives, their world, no longer will he accept an hourly slot on a Sunday morning. Unlike the old world order there is just one God and everybody is equal in his eyes.

Christmas and Easter are just as important now as they used to be but they are different. At Christmas the whole world celebrates Jesus' Birthday with him and he is the centre of the celebration, There are no presents or Christmas trees and no debt come January when the celebrating is all over. There is the ecstatic privilege of celebrating their creators Birthday.

People travel around on horseback and on donkeys and they create wooden boats to travel the lakes and water ways.

Everybody is given their own piece of land on which to grow their own fruit and vegetables. Nobody goes without and there are no taxes because everything is provided by the Lord. The only plants that are not allowed to be grown are poppies and Coca because of the underlying evil that can come from them.

Nobody eats flesh any more. Even the animals now eat plants, not each other.

The newborns soon become young adults and start their own families and after eight hundred years the population of the world has again increased into the billions. People are spread throughout the world and live in peace and harmony.

Jesus' new government is totally alien to anything the earth has ever known before. The government is there to provide for the needs of people of the new kingdom and to ensure that everyone is well cared for. There is no illness, no crime, no death and everyone is content.

A Storm on the Horizon

800 AJR (After Jesus' Return)

There has been love and peace on earth for eight hundred years now. Swallow and Te have one hundred and twenty children. Te is still a general in the army and Swallow a doting and devoted mother.

By 25 AJR new colleges and universities had started to spring up all over the world

Matthew was a second year student at college. He was studying farming and History. He was a very intelligent young man. He read his bible day after day and never doubted what it said. There was just one thing that bothered him. He could not get his head round Jesus being the son of God and Mary being a virgin.

John was finishing an essay on bible history for his college assessment. Towards the end he wrote

"I believe that Jesus was the son of God but I do not believe that Mary was a virgin."

Matthew's teacher was shocked when she read what he had written. This was unheard of. Everybody has free will to believe what they want to believe. Nobody is brainwashed on earth but this was a first in the new kingdom. Matthew's teacher blessed him for what he had written and explained that she would have to report this to the head. He wasn't punished or chastised in any way. He was given autonomy to choose his own path.

News soon got back to the Seraphim and to Jesus. Jesus had been expecting this to happen one day because he knew what was yet to come.

As news spread that Matthew had disagreed with the scriptures many more believers started to question God's word. By 950 AJR there were about 10 million non believers on earth again who now refused to worship God even.

A new police force had to be established on earth extremely quickly as this group of rebels started to talk amongst themselves.

Nobody was sure what to expect next. The Police were only there to ensure peace, not to challenge or change their beliefs. They were allowed to believe what they wanted.

The Thousand years is up

*"**7** When the thousand years are over, Satan will be released from his prison**8** and will go out to deceive the nations in the four corners of the earth—Gog and Magog—and to gather them for battle. In number they are like the sand on the seashore. **9** They marched across the breadth of the earth and surrounded the camp of God's people, the city he loves. But fire came down from heaven and devoured them. **10** And the devil, who deceived them, was thrown into the lake of burning sulphur, where the beast and the false prophet had been thrown. They will be tormented day and night forever and ever. "
Revelations 20:7-9*

1000 AJR. Day 1

As the sun rises over the Abyss the guardian angels that have kept it secure for the last thousand years start to pack away their belongings.

They start to depart to different corners of the earth and the huge grid that has covered the top of the abyss for the last thousand years starts to develop cracks in it. The guardians are busy transporting those who have been in limbo, safely away from Level 1 to the safety of Christian communities around the globe.

Suddenly there is a tremendous earthquake around the abyss and the grid cracks into three pieces, a huge chunk of it breaks off and falls into the crater which is no longer glowing with fire.

The angels have now all departed and the demons slowly start to make their way up the spiral staircase that goes up the perimeter of the abyss. They cautiously look around and see that there is nobody there.

Absinthe and his crew reach the surface. Absinthe smiles and stretches his arms above him and grins at his cronies.

"We better wait for the boss, see what the crack is."

"Bloody hell, I'm glad we're out of there", say Desparus, forcing a smile for once.

"Why they couldn't have put a lift in I'll never know" complains Sloth.

"You're complaining! I had to walk up five miles behind your sweaty fat ass Sloth!" moans Culpus

"Sssshhh, shush. He's coming now", warns Absinthe. Satan finally surfaces from the Abyss. He looks around and lets out a huge ugly roar which makes all the demons scatter back from the entrance to the abyss. He prowls around angrily.

"Get into rank the lot of you!" Satan finds an elevated spot where he can look down on his army of demons.

"The time has come for the final battle. Three thousand or so years ago we were kicked out of heaven. We were captured when Jesus returned and we've had to spend the last thousand years in that shit hall. We've got one last chance to cause as much damage as we possibly can! Get out there and target the non believers. Cocainas, Heroinas get planting your crops. Absinthe, start distilling! Desparus you and your team get ready to cause mayhem. Guerras go and start some wars. Corruptus you know what to do, the governments. Lustus get busy doing what you used to do best. I won't be far away! Gather up all the non believers for a mighty uprising!"

Satan disappears into the distance.

The demons spread themselves out over the nations yet again, for the final assault on earth.

Mika is tending his crops early one morning, The sun is in the sky and it is a lovely warm day. In the far corner of his field he notices some flowers that he has never seen before. He walks over to look at them. He picks one, it doesn't smell of much. He discards it and moves back to his vegetables, "must just be a new flower that they've introduced" he thinks to himself.

Joseph is tending his flock and he notices some new plants on his plot. He goes over to look at them, he notices their green leaves and little red berries. He doesn't think much more about it for now and carries on tending his flock.

Elsewhere in the world Corruptus and a group of demons have made their way into the government buildings to see what was going on and devise a plan to start causing disruption. They work their way through the offices invisible to the human eye, even upgraded eyed. They raid all the filing cabinets, listen in at top secret meetings and start devising a plan of action.

Mika wants to find out more about these plants so he goes to the library and gets a book out on rare plants and tree. He sits in his plot reading the book. Judging by the picture, the flower's botanical name is Papaver Somniferum.

The flower was grown mainly by poor farmers on small plots in remote regions of the world. It flourished in dry, warm climates and the vast majority of Opium poppies were grown in a narrow, 4,500-mile stretch of mountains extending across southern Asia from Turkey through Pakistan and Laos. About three months after the poppy seeds were planted; brightly coloured flowers bloomed at the tips of greenish, tubular stems. As the petals fell away, they exposed an egg-shaped seed pod. Inside the pod was an opaque, milky sap. This was Opium in its crudest form.

The sap was extracted by slitting the pod vertically in parallel strokes with a special curved knife. As the sap oozed out, it turned darker and thicker, forming a brownish-black gum. A farmer collected the gum with a scraping knife, bundled it into bricks, cakes or balls and wrapped them in a simple material such as plastic or leaves.

Then the opium entered the black market. A merchant or broker would buy the packages for transport to a morphine refinery. Most traffickers did their morphine refining close to the poppy fields, since compact morphine bricks were much easier to smuggle.

At the refinery, which was no more than a rickety laboratory equipped with oil drums and shrouded in a jungle thicket, the opium was ready for further processing into heroin.

Mika is alarmed by what he has read and is about to set fire to the flowers and wipe them out when a strong wind pick up and blows the seed heads away sending them all over the valley where they burst. Within weeks there are poppies everywhere and people are wondering what is going on. Heroinas spots some non believers near the poppy flowers and puts it in their heads to start turning the flowers into Heroin. The non believers start creating little laboratories all over the place and before long Heroin is readily available at a price.

Within weeks the first addicts emerge. An emergency police force has now been launched to stop the spread of cocaine trafficking but the demons are clever and before long hundreds of thousands of people are addicted.

Cocainas had similar success in spreading the creation of Cocaine from the Coca plants and soon the dealers were selling both.

Absinthe was having equal success distilling alcohol deep in the forest and soon it was readily available to everyone, even children.

Guerras scouted the four corners of the globe spreading dissension and hatred amongst the nations and soon political upheaval was spreading everywhere. The world was very quickly getting into a terrible state again.

Absinthe wasted no time getting people hooked again. He was turning on his charm every night and causing drunken brawls in the fields and Lustus was in full form encouraging one night stands and all sorts of other sexual exploits.

The New Jerusalem

"21Then I saw a new heaven and a new earth, for the first heaven and the first earth had passed away, and there was no longer any sea. 2 I saw the Holy City, the new Jerusalem, coming down out of heaven from God, prepared as a bride beautifully dressed for her husband. 3 And I heard a loud voice from the throne saying, "Look! God's dwelling place is now among the

people and he will dwell with them. They will be his people, and God himself will be with them and be their God. 4 'He will wipe every tear from their eyes. There will be no more death or mourning or crying or pain, for the old order of things has passed away."

5 He who was seated on the throne said, "I am making everything new!"Then he said, "Write this down, for these words are trustworthy and true." Revelation 21: 1 -5

"And I heard a loud voice from the throne saying, "Look! God's dwelling place is now among the people and he will dwell with them. They will be his people, and God himself will be with them and be their God."
Revelations 21:3

Way above the clouds the miners and the builders have completed their task of building the New Jerusalem. The city had a high wall with twelve gates and on each gate was written the name of one of the twelve tribes of Israel. There were three gates on each four sides of the cities. The wall had twelve foundations. Each foundation had a name of one of the twelve apostles of the lamb. The wall itself was made of jasper and the city itself was made of pure gold, as pure as glass. The foundations were decorated with every type of precious stone. The twelve pearls that were earlier extracted from the sea and taken above the clouds form the gates of the city. The gates of the city were made of gold as pure as transparent glass.

The city hovers over Jerusalem and now it starts to descend to the earth. The three thousand square mile structure casts an enormous shadow over the whole of the old Jerusalem, which has now been completely cleared.

Suddenly people from all over the earth see the city descending from the clouds. Many are scared and don't understand what is going on. Many others are joyful as they know that their new home with God has nearly arrived. `

On earth the police and the army are busy clearing and evacuating a three thousand square mile area from the centre of Jerusalem. The poor unsuspecting, innocent people who have lived here for a thousand years in peace with Jesus as ruler don't understand why evil has suddenly spread across the globe and why now they must evacuate their homes. Everyone is in turmoil as wars start to break everywhere.

In another part of the world children sit playing happily around a lake, totally unaware of what is going on elsewhere. A passing drug dealer has been sent by Cocainas to give out free cocaine laced sweets. He approaches the children and dishes out his deadly fare. The children eat them and start fighting with each other and shouting and fitting. He comes back the day after and the children beg him for the sweets but he tells them that they must go and steel and get money and property in exchange for them. Their parents are distraught as they don't know why their children are suddenly behaving so strangely.

The Evacuation.

The army start to organise all the believers into groups ready to enter the new Jerusalem. The city has landed on earth and the sun and moon go out of orbit, leaving the earth in complete darkness. People shuffle about trying to light fires so they can see but suddenly the earth become completely illuminated as God enter the New Jerusalem.

The army ushers everyone towards the New Jerusalem but suddenly the demons change tactics and start to physically attack the believers as they make their way towards the gates of pearl. Millions of saved people flock towards the gates. Suddenly a host of guardians dives down from the heavens and start battling with the demons to protect the believers.

The believers swarm in their millions and eventually every last one is in and the gates of the New Jerusalem close and seal for eternity.

Satan leads the hosts of demons towards the city and they surround it in their millions with the unbelievers hurling missiles at the walls of the structure but the missiles just bounce off.

Teetotaller is leading a platoon of guardian angels into battle against the demons that are attempting to stop the exile to the New Jerusalem. The order has been given to attack and defend, the gloves are off. Suddenly Te sees Absinthe attacking a believer. His eyes light up as he sees his opportunity to settle old scores. Te makes a B line for Absinthe grabbing him by the neck and landing on the ground on top of him. Straddling Absinthe he starts to let rip punching the demon in the face repeatedly. That's for Maria! That's for Pedro, that's for their baby. Absinthe is no wimp and he flicks Te off him and stands up and kicks Te in the stomach several time and then jumps up into the air and lands with his foot flat on Te's head. Te grabs his legs, kicks him in the groin and using the same leg trips Absinthe up onto the floor and pins him there in a wrestling style leg lock and then grabs at Absinthe's neck and pulls his head right back. "You bastard Absinthe I've waited a long time for this opportunity,"

"Come on old pal let's not fight like children, let's go and talk about it over a drink"

"I'm not your Pal" Suddenly the earth behind Absinthe parts and lava starts to come out of the earth behind him. In an incredible display of strength Te stands up and lifts Absinthe up into the air with both hands. He manoeuvres Absinthe over the lava pit and throws him in. Absinthe sets on fire and screams in agony as the lava devours him. Te collapses onto the ground by the lava pit, cut and bruised. His arch enemy is now gone for eternity.

The Lake of Burning Sulphur.

"11 Then I saw a great white throne and him who was seated on it. The earth and the heavens fled from his presence, and there was no place for them. 12 And I saw the dead, great and small, standing before the throne, and books were opened. Another book was opened, which is the book of life. The dead were judged according to what they had done as recorded in the books. 13 The sea gave up the dead that were in it, and death and Hades gave up the dead that were in them, and each person was judged according to what they had done. 14 Then death and Hades were thrown into the lake of fire. The lake of fire is the second death. 15 Anyone whose name was not found written in the book of life was thrown into the lake of fire."
Revelation 20:11-14

Suddenly there is a blinding flash and the whole earth apart from the New Jerusalem erupts into a mighty and violent earthquake. Lava starts to seethe from the cracks that are forming in the earth's crust until the whole earth is nothing but a mound of molten lava. Satan, the demons and those who during the thousand years chose not to believe are devoured for eternity into the lake of burning sulphur. Lustus, Desparus, Metus, Culpus, Sloth and Suicidus all scream in agony and terror as the lava devours them and they all disappear, never to be seen again. Heroinas, Cocainas and their followers the drug dealers all meet their doom in the lake of burning sulphur.

The celebration

A new era has emerged. After the final judgement God and his people have finally been united on earth and all evil and sinfulness is completely locked out forever. The millions of believers gather for a huge celebration. The saved of the churches from all the nations gather to sings praises to God. A hundred square mile choir of musicians gather. Millions upon millions of believers sing "Holy Holy Holy Lord God Almighty". The throne and the end of the golden road are lit up as bright as lightning. The Stars of this 3050 year story of pride, disobedience, dissension, sadness, loss, hope, freedom and unconditional love start to walk down the golden road towards the throne. First up are Seth, Enos, and kenan, Mahalale, Jared, Enoch, Methuselah, Lamech, Noah and Shem. The crowds applaud as they make their way down the golden road towards the throne of God.

Next up are the ancestors of the twelve tribes of Israel. Jacob followed by Asher, Benjamin, Dan, Gad, Issachar, Joseph, Tribe of Menasheh, Judah, Levi,Naphtali, Reuben, Simeon, Tribe of Ephraim, tribe of Menasheh, Judah, Levi, Naphtali, Reuben, Simeon and Zebulun. Then the apostles -

Peter, Andrew, James, son of zebedee, John the evangelist, Philip, Bartholomew, Thomas, Matthew, John son of Alphaeus, Judas son of James and Simon the Canaanite and Matthias, who replaced Judas Iscariot and also

Paul Titus and Mary Magdalene. Next up are the disciples of Jesus who receive an astounding applause as they make their way down the golden road towards the throne.

Penultimately, Mary and Joseph, Jesus' parents walk hand in hand towards the throne and behind them, their precious son, and our Saviour Jesus Christ walks down the golden road to sit beside his heavenly father.

The singing and praising goes on for weeks during which there is a feast like no other feast.

Background to the Characters

Satan – Née Lucifer. Was God's bodyguard and the most perfect and beautiful of all the Angels at one time? His pride got him booted out of Heaven.

Absinthe – Née Acqua. Was a good friend of Lucifer in the heavenly realms before God created the earth? He was responsible for providing drinking water to all the Angels in the heavenly realms.

Desparus - Née Gaudium maintained contentment and happiness in the heavenly realms. He was everyone's nurturing parent and if any of the angels had a problem they would go to him for a listening ear. When Gaudium chose to leave heaven with Lucifer he was replaced by another angel.

Metus - Née Animus was the angel in charge of promoting courage and fearlessness amongst the hosts of angels. A mighty warrior angel. When he chose to follow Satan he became his alter ego Metus, charged with instilling fear in anybody who was vulnerable.

Culpus - Née Insontis was the angel of innocence. When he was booted out of heaven with Lucifer he became responsible for hounding the vulnerable with extreme guilt. Guilt way beyond conscience.

Lustus – Née Sanctimonia was the angel of purity. This angel was replaced before he left heaven, as soon as there was even a shadow of a doubt about his allegiance to God, as no impurity is ever to be found in the heavenly realms.

Suicidus - Née Vita. Vita was responsible for promoting healthy lifestyles and fitness amongst the angels. He was so energetic he used to run bums and tums classes and Zumba groups for the angels. When he was kicked out with Lucifer he became Suicidus, his alter ego, responsible for convincing as many of the human race to take their lives as possible. His home on was the Aokigahara Forest in Japan at the base of Mount Fiji. Right up until the day Jesus returned this forest was renowned for being a place where people went to take their own lives.

Alex Floss was born in Alabama USA. One of six children, he was the brightest in his class at high school and graduated from Harvard University with his first degree in psychology and then did his MA and Ph.D. in psychological profiling At Harvard University. From here he went on to a successful career as a psychological profiler for the FBI. He solved many famous cases and even worked as a consultant on the Hannibal Lector case. He was saved in his teens at his local Baptist church and served in his local church all his life as a steward. He entered the New Jerusalem with Swallow,

Te, Petrova and his wife Patricia and four of their six children.

Helga Petrova was born in Kiev, Russia. She was the youngest of four children born into a wealthy family. Orphaned at two months old when her parents were killed in a plane crash. Her grandparents brought her up until she was fourteen when her grandmother died of alcohol poisoning. She was then sent to live in the US with her aunt and despite never getting over the death of her grandmother until well into her thirties she excelled at law school and went on to a successful career as a lawyer and then District Attorney. She married and had two children with her first husband and then left him quite controversially for a local politician who she eventually married and had another two children with.

Agent Swallow was born in New Jersey. First born of three children, she grew up in a very poor family. She was a hard worker at school and excelled throughout her studies at school, college and university she then went straight into the FBI as an undergraduate and did her degree through the FBI. Her most famous case was Hannibal Lector, who she never caught.

Angel Gabriel was a messenger. He was Archangel Michael's brother. He was one of God's most loyal and trusted angels. Once the New Jerusalem was established on earth Gabriel was given his own fishing lake, boat house and boat to spend eternity enjoying a peaceful life.

Teetotaller – Née Curatio was a guardian Angel. He spent all his working life looking after his protégés on earth. Then he humanized to testify against Absinthe but his main reason for doing so was to marry Swallow.

Justicius – was a bounty hunter. Before the return of Jesus he was a body guard for the Seraphim.

Albert the Pub Landlord was born in Burnley, Lancashire, England. He was one of three brothers and his parents worked in the mills. He was saved but was reprimanded for his involvement in the death of Mark and his friends, for not doing anything about the situation.

"I have an analogy for you - You're a "tennis ball"! Sounds crazy that doesn't it! Well think of it like this – there are four Demons (Mindsets, if you want to be less superstitious) playing tennis with you, only they are not trying to catch each other out, as in traditional tennis and this game is not played on a traditional tennis court. This game is played within your Mind, Will and Emotions. They are deliberately passing you from one player to the next. Anxiety has first serve (usually at around the same time every day), it smacks you over to Fear. Fear in turn belts you over to Alcohol and then Alcohol pounds you right back over to Desperation. This game starts at roughly the same time every day for an Alcoholic, sometimes it never ends but the players change. Fear might sit out while Guilt stretches its legs and then, who knows, Guilt might have a rest while Anxiety has a go."
Four funerals and a revelation, Cook AW.2006

This notion of demons using addicts as the ball came to me when I was writing my second book back in 2006 about my own experiences with addiction.

Fictional characters like Maria, Bill, Helen and the young man killed in the bus crash really do exist in the world that we live in. Addiction- whether it is to alcohol or drugs follows the same pattern for addicts, over and over again.

I got the notion of Absinthe being the great entertainer because when you're drunk or high you don't worry, you are distracted and after all entertainment is simply a distraction, whatever shape or form it takes. Metus, Culpus and

Desparus – fear, guilt and despair are emotions and feelings that are common to every single addict. They may be there before the addiction comes along or the addiction may come along to keep despair, fear and guilt at bay or they may emerge after the addiction has taken a grip.

I was inspired by films such as 'Goodfellas' and 'The Untouchables' because the violent, nasty characters in those films do run rackets and dominate people with fear and violence. I intended to show how these emotions and feelings work in a vicious cycle that keeps the addict paralysed in a state of despair – fear – guilt – temporary relief, this cycle continues over and over again until one of two things happens. A. The addict manages to break free from the addiction, either on their own or through an intervention or B. the natural consequences of addiction such as death from a related illness, suicide or an accident finally occur.

"**23** for the wages of sin is death; but the gift of God is eternal life through Jesus Christ our Lord. "

Romans 6:23

My musical inspiration throughout this book has been first and foremost 'Vide Cor Meum' predominantly the version used in the film 'Hannibal'. It's a beautiful, relaxing piece of music that makes it easy to imagine the hosts of God's angels as they are going about doing what they do.

I got my inspiration for the investigators from the films 'Along came a spider' and 'Kiss the Girls'. Alex floss is Alex Cross the forensic psychologist. Agent Swallow, if you've not guest it already is Clarice Starling from 'Silence of the

Lambs' was a bit of a tongue in cheek kind of name. They seemed to fit perfectly for the investigation and Swallow was a prime candidate for some romance as she was young, single, pretty and good looking. Teetotaller's letter to Swallow was a real letter, written by someone, for someone, but never sent.

The song that inspired that letter was 'Unchained melody'. The tragedy throughout the whole story is that this void, this desire for something unknown, that as humans we can never really define or put our finger on is our need for relationship with our creator God. Until we know him we spend our lives trying to fill that void with whatever fits for the moment. The novelty inevitably wears off and we end up searching again and again. The world in which we live bombards us with ways to temporarily fill that void, just watch the adverts between Coronation Street and you'll be given plenty of options, plus our Internet, magazines and books are full of shallow 'stuff' to fill the void with. Alcohol and drugs are extreme tactics used by Satan to ensnare us and he is very subtle and crafty the way he goes about it.

The underlying truth behind this story is the subtle power of addiction, any addiction and the reason for it which is man's search for relationship with his God and escape from the traumas of life. On top of that, the hope we have, if we believe, that one day there will be no more hatred, no more pain, no more addictions, war, violence and everything else that Satan has thrown at us since his eviction from heaven.

Made in the USA
Charleston, SC
01 May 2013